ADVANCES IN SMALL BUSINESS FINANCE

FINANCIAL AND MONETARY POLICY STUDIES

Volume 21

The titles published in this series are listed at the end of this volume.

ADVANCES IN
SMALL BUSINESS FINANCE

Edited by

RASSOUL YAZDIPOUR

California State University,
Fresno, California, U.S.A.

With a Foreword
by
David A. Walker

Kluwer Academic Publishers
Dordrecht / Boston / London

Library of Congress Cataloging-in-Publication Data

Advances in small business finance / edited by Rassoul Yazdipour ;
foreword by David A. Walker.
    p.   cm. -- (Financial and monetary policy studies ; v. 21)
  "Chosen ... from ... papers accepted for presentation at the First
Annual Small Firm Financial Research Symposium held at California
State University, Fresno ... in 1989"--Pref.
  ISBN 0-7923-1135-3 (HB : acid-free paper)
  1. Small business--Finance--Congresses.   I. Yazdipour, Rassoul,
1951-   . II. Small Firm Financial Research Symposium (1st : 1989 :
California State University, Fresno)   III. Series: Financial and
monetary policy studies ; 21.
HG4027.7.A34 1991
658.15'92--dc20   91-4367

ISBN 0-7923-1135-3

Published by Kluwer Academic Publishers,
P.O. Box 17, 3300 AA Dordrecht, The Netherlands.

Kluwer Academic Publishers incorporates
the publishing programmes of
D. Reidel, Martinus Nijhoff, Dr W. Junk and MTP Press.

Sold and distributed in the U.S.A. and Canada
by Kluwer Academic Publishers,
101 Philip Drive, Norwell, MA 02061, U.S.A.

In all other countries, sold and distributed
by Kluwer Academic Publishers Group,
P.O. Box 322, 3300 AH Dordrecht, The Netherlands.

Printed on acid-free paper

Printed in the Netherlands

To:

Joseph J. Penbera,
a man of great vision

Table of contents

viii

FOREWORD

Small business research is becoming more sophisticated as an increasing number of scholars study more complex analytical issues. In many cases research pertaining to the small firm is part of the incomplete and inefficient markets controversy in the finance literature. Because of their size and traditional organizational form, small firms often find it extremely difficult to attract significant resources in sophisticated financial markets. These markets appear to be segmented and incomplete; whether or not the markets are efficient is subject to much debate. Advances in Small Business Finance presents a variety of research studies that indicate the unique roles of debt and equity and the sources of funds for small firms. This book contributes important insight into major questions that face small firms' financiers, managers, and owners on a daily basis.

Many of the studies in this volume deal with aspects of valuation of the small firm. In some instances, the focus is on the firm's ability to attract debt or equity and in others the emphasis is on valuation of the small firm's capital.

Constand, Osteryoung, and Nast focus on the determinants of capital structure for small firms that are privately owned and are highly dependent on commercial loans as their supply of debt. Timothy Bates examines firm viability and finds that surviving firms are those that began with greater initial capital, create new jobs, and are led by entrepreneurs who are better educated.

Buck, Friedman, and Dunkelberg examine risk-return tradeoffs and lending decisions for banks that lend to small firms in various phases of a business cycle; as macro-economic uncertainty increases in global markets, the focus of this paper is a current concern for most small firms. Harry Guenther analyzes the effects of recent banking regulation and legislative initiatives on the availability of funds to finance small firms; he finds that recent banking regulations may have some adverse effects on the supply and costs of funds for small firms.

Osteryoung, Nast and Wells develop a framework for measuring minority discounts in valuing closely-held firms, which is an economic issue that is considered in many law cases; they argue that discounts must be determined by financial theory and analysis rather than arbitrary approaches that have often been employed. Krinsky and Rotenberg critique several of the highly regarded empirical studies on valuation of initial public offerings using Canadian data that distinguishes between large and small issuing firms; they find that high book values of assets prior to the offering are a primary determinant of initial public value. Easterwood and Singer examine the motives for taking large and small firms private; they find that firm size affects the motivation and that small firm buyouts are often undertaken to reduce stockholder servicing costs and owner-manager conflicts.

Edward Dyl describes franchising as an important organizational form to enable entrepreneurs to begin new ventures; he shows that franchising is a market solution to support origination and development of small firms while reducing agency costs. David Walker presents an empirical analysis of a model that delineates relationships among the sources of financing the small firm; he emphasizes the need for expanded databases and further empirical work on small business models. Charles Ou provides an important survey of information on financing small business for current and future research.

Many of the issues that face small business are fundamental questions that influence the performance of the U.S. economy since small firms employ more than half of the labor force and produce a large share of the national output. Expanding the financial resources for small firms to survive or to grow into major firms is a public policy issue that legislative bodies and public agencies must focus on if the U.S. is to continue its sustained economic growth in the 1990s. The development of small firms also affects many large firms because they subcontract to small firms or depend on them for major inputs.

Advances in Small Business Finance should stimulate other studies that will provide insight into the issues that small firms face in their efforts to develop into major enterprises. The variety of papers presented in this volume should appeal to a wide audience.

This volume is the result of much diligent management by Professor Rassoul Yazdipour of California State University at Fresno. Rassoul has led the evolution of the Small Firm Financial Research Symposium, at which the papers in this volume were first presented, and he has undertaken the editorship of a new small business finance journal that will present scholarly papers.

David A. Walker

PREFACE

Small business finance, as an emerging and promising field of study, has recently received a great deal of attention from researchers and specialists from all over the world. A quick look at the list of references provided at the end of this book in Appendix A, as well as the level and types of issues raised and examined in this present volume, reveals this fact. In addition to the advancements made in the field so far, there is little doubt that such a trend will continue in the future[1].

There are at least four major reasons that the field of small business finance is gaining more recognition and acceptance among scholars and professionals world-wide. These reasons can be listed as follows.

1- The prevalence of a trend that has become known as "defirming" of the public corporation. As Kensinger and Martin (1989) report[2], over the 1985-1989 period, 143 corporations have disappeared from the Fortune 500 list and many others have gone through significant downsizing.

2- The availability of new financial data bases at the micro level. Appendix B at the end of this book provides a listing of some of the available databases in the area of small business. Some of the chapters in this book will also provide more insight into the available data sources.

3- The emergence of new financial markets such as the $ 33 Billion U.S. formal venture capital market[3], the $ 56-Billion-a-year informal venture capital market[4] (U.S.), and the recently created "144a market"; as well as new financing methods and instruments- like Employee Stock Ownership Plans (ESOPs).

4- The general trend, especially in the U.S., toward entrepreneurship and small business. The nature and speed of recent technological developments as well as the wave of corporate restructurings in the 1980s, and the accompanying corporate job insecurities, have all made the trend toward entrepreneurship inevitable.

Regardless of any other consideration, small businesses represent a very important segment of all economies. For example, at the end of 1987, 47% of all the U.S. assets were under management by smaller businesses[5] and the small firms' contribution to U.S. output was 50% in 1982, the most recent year for which data is available[6]. Also, half of the total sales receipts are generated by small businesses and the majority of new jobs are created by such companies.

The objective of this book is to present to readers the products of some of the recent research activities carried out in the growing field of small business finance. In doing so, it is hoped that more researchers will get involved in the process and further help to raise the degree of efficiency of the financial markets in which small business owners, investors, and managers operate.

The articles included in this volume were chosen, through a referee process, from among the papers accepted for presentation at the First Annual Small Firm Financial Research

Symposium held at California State University, Fresno, California, in 1989. Such a symposium, the first of its kind, was sponsored by California State University, Fresno and Wells Fargo Bank. A complete copy of the program of this symposium, as well as the program for the 1990 symposium, is provided in Appendix C at the end of this book. I would like to take this opportunity to thank the contributors to this volume for their work and cooperation in making it possible for this collection to be published. Much appreciation also goes to Wells Fargo Bank for their contribution to the Symposium.

The intended readers of this volume include researchers and professionals involved in different areas of investment and "corporate" finance. This book is also particularly useful to government officials and policymakers dealing with different issues related to small businesses. The present collection is also very appropriate as a reading book for graduate students in the areas of business finance and economics.

Rassoul Yazdipour
Summer 1990
Fresno, California

Endnotes

1. Evidence is the resounding success of the first three Annual Small Firm Financial Research Symposia. The Program for the last two conferences is provided in Appendix C at the end of this book.

2. John W. Kensinger and John D. Martin, (November/December 1989), 'The Decline of Public Equity: The Return to Private Enterprise?', Business Horizons, page 14.

3. See Venture Capital Journal, (April 1990), 'Special Report', page 11. This trade journal published by Venture Economics, Inc., Needham, Massachusetts.

4. See Robert Gaston, (1989), 'The Scale of Informal Capital Markets', Small Business Economics: An International Journal, 223-230.

5. See The State of Small Business: A Report of the President, 1989, U.S. Small Business Administration, Washington, D.C., Page 126.

6. Ibid, Page xiii.

ACKNOWLEDGEMENTS

Special appreciation and gratitude goes to members of the Review Board of the First Annual Small Firm Financial Research Symposium:

James S. Ang, *Florida State University*
K.C. Chen, *California State University, Fresno*
Thomas A. Gray, *Small Business Administration*
Dewey E. Johnson, *California State University, Fresno*
Herbert L. Lyken, *University of Massachusetts, Boston*
John D. Martin, *University of Texas*
William Petty, Abilene *Christian University*
Charles C.F. Ou, *Small Business Administration*
Lemma W. Senbet, *University of Wisconsin-Madison*
Donald Shannon, *DePaul University*
Gary C. Sanger, *Louisiana State University*
Hans Schollhammer, *University of California, Los Angeles*
David A. Walker, *Georgetown University*

To Professors Jerome S. Osteryoung, J. William Petty, David A. Walker and Dr. Charles Ou, I want to say thank you so much for all the help and the encouragement you provided me.

Special thanks and appreciation also goes to my colleagues, especially, Professors Paul M. Lange, Joseph W. Wilson, K. C. Chen, A. Rufus Waters, Dewey E. Johnson and Elizabeth M. Shields. Professors Paul Lange and Joseph Wilson went out of their way in supporting the symposium idea.

Also, thanks to Professors David P. Ely (San Diego State University), Robert Kieschnick (University of Manitoba), John E. Young (University of New Mexico), and Janis K. Zaima (San Jose State University) for their help in reviewing some of the submitted papers.

Lastly, but not the least, I much appreciate the efforts of my former assistant, Rosalind M. McCoy, and my new assistants, Winnie Yip and Ken Chan whose hard work and diligence made my job much easier. Also, many thanks to Karen Linville for her much helpful administrative support.

THE VALUATION OF INITIAL PUBLIC OFFERINGS :
THE SMALL FIRM CASE*

I. KRINSKY
Faculty of Business
McMaster University,
Hamilton, Ontario L8S 4M4
Canada

W. ROTEBERG
Faculty of Business
McMaster University,
Hamilton, Ontario L8S 4M4
Canada

ABSTRACT. This study provides empirical evidence on the relationships between initial firm value, actions taken by entrepreneurs and information revealed in the offering prospectus for small and large firms. Empirical specifications employed in previous studies are first re-estimated and it is shown that after adjusting for heteroskedasticity, most of the results can not be validated. In particular, we do not detect a significant coefficient for the entrepreneurial ownership retention signal in any specification, although it is of the predicted sign. The study explicitly distinguishes between initial public offerings of large and small firms to determine whether there are size related biases in the capital acquisition process. Although larger firms pay a smaller portion of total issue proceeds in underwriting fees, this is explained by issue characteristics other than firm size. Key variables include the size of the issue, the nature of the offering and the availability of historical financial data in the offering prospectus. The proportion of total proceeds paid to underwriters is then included as an additional signal in the valuation model. An inverse relationship is detected between initial firm value and underwriting fees, supporting the notion that the underwriting fee schedule has information content. For all definitions of initial value employed (market vs. subscription prices), and after controlling for other information available to investors, initial value is found to be significantly higher for firms with a high book value of assets prior to the offering.

* This study was supported in part by the Accounting Research and Education Center, McMaster University. The authors would like to thank the participants at the Small Firm Financial Research Symposium, Fresno, 1989, for their valuable comments.

1

R. Yazdipour (ed.), Advances in Small Business Finance, 1–18.
© 1991 *Kluwer Academic Publishers. Printed in the Netherlands.*

1. Introduction

The theoretical models[1] dealing with signalling and the valuation of unseasoned common shares are rich relative to the few empirical papers investigating these relationships (e.g. Downes and Heinkel, 1982; Ritter, 1984; Simunic and Stein, 1987; Beatty, 1987; Tinic, 1988; Krinsky and Rotenberg, 1989). The limited empirical work on initial public offerings (IPO's) might be due to the difficulty in formulating testable hypotheses based on the currently available theoretical models. Further, none of the empirical studies has focused on comparing IPO's by large and small companies. This is surprising, given the evidence of systematic differences in the performance of seasoned shares of large and small firms. Several explanations have been offered for this phenomenon, which is generally referred to as the "small firm effect". Examples include possible misspecification of betas (Roll, 1981; Barry and Brown, 1985), use of an improper market index (Thaler 1987), and the differential information hypothesis (Barry and Brown, 1984, 1985; Klein and Bawa, 1977)[2]. In particular, the latter may be of interest in the IPO context. Information differentials for large and small firms might be reflected in the valuation of unseasoned common shares.

It is the purpose of this paper to examine the relationships between initial firm value, potential actions by entrepreneurs and various pieces of information revealed in the offering prospectus for large and small companies. In what follows, the next section describes previous empirical studies. The data set from the Toronto Stock Exchange (TSE) which is used to avoid the danger of "data snooping" (Lakonishok and Smidt, 1989) is also described. Empirical results obtained by re-estimating the Downes and Heinkel (1982) and Ritter (1984) models are discussed in the fourth section. The study explicitly distinguishes between large and small firms with the aim of identifying issue characteristics which might explain differences in underwriting fees and valuation. Section five provides an alternative model specification which is tested using data for large and small issuing firms and our findings are summarized in the sixth and final section.

2. Previous Studies

Leland and Pyle (1977) construct a univariate financial signalling model in the context of the CAPM in which the current value of the firm, V, is a function of α -- the fraction of equity retained by the entrepreneur. Investors perceive the selected signal to be credible, because the signal is costly (in terms of suboptimal diversification) and the marginal cost of false signalling exceeds the marginal benefit. Thus, the entrepreneur's willingness to invest serves as a signal of expected project value.[3] Based on the Leland and Pyle model, the value of the firm is given by:

$$V(\alpha) = \frac{[-bZ]}{(1+r)} \hat{\alpha} + K \tag{1}$$

where:

r = the risk-free rate of interest,

b = the risk aversion of the entrepreneur, expressed as a parameter in a mean-variance utility function,

K = the amount of capital raised in the initial offer, and

Z = the project specific risk, which is a function of the return to the firm and the market.

The Leland and Pyle (LP) signal of the firm's future cashflow, $\hat{\alpha}$, is equal to $\alpha + 1n\,(1 - \alpha)$. By observing α, and given knowledge of the other parameters, investors are able to derive the true value of the firm. In their test of the LP model, Downes and Heinkel (1982) use the following regression line to express firm j's value:

$$V_j = b_0 + b_1 K_j + b_2 \hat{\alpha}_j + u_j \qquad (2)$$

This specification implicitly assumes that the risk measure, Z, is constant across all firms in the sample. Further, since $dV/d\alpha < 0$ [equation (1)], one would expect b_2 [equation (2)] to be negative. Downes and Heinkel find that firms do have higher value where the fraction of ownership retained by the entrepreneur is high.[4] No attempt is made to distinguish among companies on the basis of size. One might suspect that the sample screening procedure employed in the study served to eliminate most of the small firms.[5,6]

Communication by direct disclosures (e.g. through accounting reports) is usually dismissed due to potential moral hazard problems. Nevertheless, Downes and Heinkel (1982), and Ritter (1984) find pre-IPO reported sales and earnings to be highly significant in explaining market values of firms undertaking initial stock offerings. Motivated by these findings, Hughes (1986) incorporates direct disclosure as an additional signal in her model. The credibility of the direct disclosure as a signal is derived from the threat of future litigation if actual performance is significantly lower than projected. In her framework, the entrepreneur reveals two pieces of information about the distribution of the firm's expected future cash flows. A risk-neutral investment banking syndicate acts as the intermediary between the entrepreneur and outside investors, receiving compensation which exactly offsets the costs of investigating and guaranteeing the accuracy of information disclosed.

The role of intermediaries in IPO's is also examined by Titman and Trueman (1986). In their model, the quality of auditors is used by investors in assessing the value of new shares.[7] The quality of an investment banker or auditor is described in terms of the amount and accuracy of information supplied to investors. The higher the quality of the information provider, the more accurately can capital suppliers estimate a firm's future cash flows. Thus, an owner with favorable projects will select a higher quality banker and the higher the quality, the higher the price at which the new issue can be sold and the greater the initial value of the firm. The Leland and Pyle signal (i.e., the percentage of ownership retained) appears only implicitly in this model since it is assumed to be determined exogenously by factors unrelated to the entrepreneur's private information.[8]

3. Data Description

The 115 new listings on the TSE which comprise the sample for this study are identical to the ones in Krinsky and Rotenberg (1989). The sample is broken down into two subsamples on the basis of the book value of assets prior to the offering. Firms are classified as small if their asset value was below $10 million. In total, 63 companies were classified as "small" using this criterion. Data extracted from the prospectuses include firms' initial market values, financial disclosures, the proposed use of proceeds from the stock issue and the distribution

TABLE 1. Sample Characteristics

Distribution of Issue Proceeds

	Mean ($000)	Percent of total
Total Proceeds	$15,423	100
Issue Expenses	152	1
Underwriting Fees	921	6
Entrepreneur	1,542	10
Net Proceeds to Firm	12,838	83

Number of Years of Historical Financial Data Disclosed

Number of Years	Frequency	Percent
0	4	3.5
1	22	19.1
2	10	8.7
3	12	10.4
4	26	22.6
5	41	35.7

of shareholdings subsequent to the issue. Additional items relating to the underwriter, such as his identity and underwriting fees, were also obtained.

In addition to information on the distribution of issue proceeds, Table 1 contains a description of the number of years of historical financial data available. The majority of the new issues disclose more than three years of financial statements. In any initial offering, only a portion of the issue proceeds is actually used by the firm for new investments or the reduction of other financing sources. The remainder is either spent on underwriting fees (6 percent) and issue expenses (1 percent) or is removed from the firm by the entrepreneur for his personal use (10 percent). In the current sample, on average, 83 percent of issue proceeds are made available to the firm.

The reported values of total assets, sales revenue and net earnings in the year prior to issue were collected for each firm. Average values and their cross-sectional variability are presented in Table 2 for the two subsamples. These data are used in testing the relevance of direct accounting disclosures in evaluating initial public offerings. In Table 2 we also report the average first day and first week market returns. On the surface, it seems that our sample is subject to the same underpricing phenomenon reported in earlier studies (see, for example, Logue, 1973; Ibbotson, 1975; Beatty and Ritter, 1986 and Tinic, 1988). Using a rank test[9] (see Table 3), no difference was found between the initial after market performance of "small" and "large" IPO's. A rank test also indicates that there is a significant difference in the magnitude of the LP signal for the two subsamples (see Table 3).

TABLE 2. Financial Disclosures in the Year Prior to Issue and Initial Market Returns

	Total Sample		Small Firms		Large Firms	
	Mean	Std. dev.	Mean	Std. dev.	Mean	Std. dev.
Total Assets ($000)	35,794	102,000	3,848	2,926	73,165	141,980
Sales Revenue ($000)	27,855	80,893	8,986	22,177	50,875	114,470
Net Income ($000)	251	8,427	542	1,192	-104	12,547
Day 1 Return (%)	11.6	40.2	11.1	46.4	12.2	31.9
Week 1 Return (%)	9.9	40.2	8.8	46.2	11.2	32.1

TABLE 3. Rank Tests Size(0,1) vs. Issue Characteristics

Characteristic	|Z|	2-tail P
UNDPER	2.046	.041
Day 1 Market Return	1.173	.241
Week 1 Market Return	1.451	.147
LP signal	2.124	.034

Underwriter "quality" was determined using the Financial Post ranking of investment dealers.[10] Of the 35 underwriters in our sample, 18 firms which were ranked in the top 10 at least once during the 1982 to 1985 period are classified as "high quality" or "prestigious".

To further characterize the role of underwriters as information providers, the fees charged for underwriting services are examined. The underwriting costs are expected to be related to issue characteristics. For example, one might argue that underwriting costs increase with underwriting risk. This differs from Hughes (1986) who, in justifying the risk neutrality assumption, argues that a syndicate of investment bankers is formed in firm commitment underwriting agreements. While correct in the general sense, most lead underwriters in our sample underwrite a large portion of the issue.[11]

Hence, the fraction of underwriting costs as a percentage of the total proceeds of the issue may serve as an additional signal to outsiders regarding the quality of the issue. The proportion of total proceeds paid for underwriting services (net of issue expenses) for the jth initial offering - $UNDPER_j$ is used as a measure of underwriting costs. The rank test indicates that smaller firms pay significantly more for underwriting services than their larger counterparts (Table 3).

4. Emprical Results Revisited

For ease of comparison, the results obtained by Downes and Heinkel (1982) are presented in Table 4 on lines (1) - (3). The total market value of equity after the IPO, V, is measured as

TABLE 4. Test of the LP Model-Downes and Heinkel (1982)[ψ]

$$V_j = b_0 + b_1 K_j + b_2 \alpha_j + u_j$$

Sample	Estimation Method	Weighting Factor	x10^7 b_0	b_1	x10^7 b_2
(1) DH	OLS	—	-17.05 (1.81)*	4.17 (.42)*	-42.31 (3.05)*
(2) DH	WLS	$1\sqrt{K_j}$	-.49 (.55)	3.52 (.24)*	-4.24 (.83)*
(3) DH	WLS	$1\sqrt{B_j}$	-.87 (.54)	2.92 (.40)*	-4.72 (.91)*
(4) TSE	OLS	—	.055 (.021)*	-1.01 (1.90)	-.023 (.010)*
(5) TSE	WLS	$1\sqrt{K_j}$	.045 (.018)*	-.79 (.52)	-.016 (.010)
(6) TSE	WLS	$1\sqrt{B_j}$	.041 (.016)*	-.71 (.59)	-.015 (.007)*
(7) TSE	OLS'	—	.055 (.048)	-1.01 (1.33)	-.023 (.021)
(8) TSE Small Subsample	OLS'	—	.006 (.006)	.236 (.24)	-.002 (.003)

ψ   Standard errors in parentheses.
OLS'   Standard errors estimated with White's (1980) heteroskedasticity consistent covariance matrix.
*   Significant at the 5 percent level.

the subscription price per share multiplied by the number of shares outstanding after the initial offer. The investment variable, K, is measured as the offer price multiplied by the number of shares issued. Thus, it does not take into account the difference between gross issue proceeds and the net proceeds made available to the firm. In model (1), OLS estimation is used. In Models (2) and (3), the weighting factors employed in the WLS estimation procedure are K and B (the issue proceeds and the book value of the firm after the new issue, respectively). In all three models, the LP signal has the predicted sign and is statistically significant. We reestimate the Downes and Heinkel model using the TSE data set (Table 4, lines 4 - 8). The results indicate that the LP signal has the predicted negative coefficient in all models.[12]

Since significant heteroskedasticity is present, in models (7) and (8) White's (1980) heteroskedasticity consistent estimate of the variance matrix is used in computing standard errors. Model (7) is estimated using the full TSE sample while Model (8) is estimated using the subsample containing only "small" firms. The White (1980) approach is less restrictive than WLS as no assumptions are required about the variation of the disturbance term. By using WLS to overcome the heteroskedasticity problem, in models (2), (3), (5) and (6), one is assuming that the variance of the disturbance term is proportional to the square of one of the explanatory variables.[13] As the LP signal is not significant in Models (7) and (8), the generality of the Downes and Heinkel results is questionable and the significance of the LP signal might be attributed to the specific assumptions utilized in estimating these models.

Alternative specifications which utilized closing prices from the first trading day produce similar results. In general, one should prefer using the market price in measuring the dependent variable. The subscription price requires a "rational expectations" assumption which may be inappropriate, given existing evidence (cited earlier) on the underpricing of unseasoned shares.[14]

Hughes (1989) argues that the LP signal (equation (1)) implicitly assumes constant end of period cash flows across sample firms. In order to at least partially relax this assumption, he proposes a decomposition of the firm specific risk into a return component, assumed to be constant across all firms, and a firm-specific value component. That is, the firm specific component of end of period cash flows can be decomposed into a rate of return variance, σ_r^2 (assumed to be constant), and a function of initial market value (equation (3)):

$$\sigma^2 = V^2 \sigma_r^2 \tag{3}$$

The substitution of equation (3) into the LP model (equation (1)) results in the following specification:

$$\frac{(V_j - K_j)}{V_j^2} = \beta_0 + \beta_1 \hat{\alpha}_j + u_j \tag{4}$$

where the dependent variable is described as the (scaled) excess of value over investment. Consistent with the results obtained using the Downes Heinkel model (equation (2)), the LP signal remains insignificant for the whole sample, as well as for the subsample of "small" firms, when this specification is employed.[15] These results differ markedly from those obtained by Hughes (1989). This is not surprising, since Hughes uses the same U.S. data as Downes and Heinkel, and his findings might be attributed to "data snooping".

Next, the competing hypotheses suggested by Ritter are tested. To raise a given amount of money, initial owners of firms with greater market values must sell a smaller proportion of their holdings. According to Ritter's wealth effect hypothesis, this relationship will cause the coefficient on the insider ownership retention variable (a_1 in equation (5) below) to be accentuated when OLS estimation is employed. The suggested valuation model is:

$$V_j = a_0 + a_1 \alpha_j + a_2 E_j + a_3 I_j + u_j \tag{5}$$

where:

V_j = initial firm value, measured as the post-offering market value of equity,

α_j = the proportion of ownership retained by insiders,
E_j = the annual earnings of the firm for the year prior to going public, and
I_j = the net proceeds raised by the firm in the IPO.

All variables are expressed in constant dollar terms. In addition, Ritter suggests the inclusion of the predicted, rather than the actual, proportion of ownership retained as an alternative specification of equation (5). The predicted value of a is estimated using the following equation:

$$\alpha_j = b_0 + b_1 V_j + b_2 E_j + b_3 \ln SG_j + u_j \tag{6}$$

where:
$\ln SG$ = the log of the sales growth rate.

Ritter's results are presented in Table 5, Rows 1 and 2. As expected, a_1 is positive and statistically significant, but the two-stage estimation procedure results in an increase, rather than a decrease, in a_1 (equation (5)). The wealth effect hypothesis is also not supported when our data set is used. The a_1 coefficient is insignificant and negative in both specifications for the whole sample (Rows 3 and 4 of Table 5). When the sample is broken down into "large" and "small" firms, however, the coefficient remains negative but becomes significant. Further, it is smaller when the two-stage estimation procedure is employed. A Chow (1960) test indicates that the "small" firms do not obey the same relationship as the "large".[16] In short, as in the original study, the wealth effect hypothesis does not receive empirical support, but for different reasons.

Under the agency hypothesis, the lower the fraction of insider holdings, the lower will be firm value, since managerial shirking reduces the firms' cash flows. Accordingly, in regressions with α as the dependent variable (equation (6)), the coefficient on relative firm value (b_1) will be overstated. Ritter also suggests a two stage estimation procedure to examine this hypothesis. Equation (5) is used to calculate the predicted market value of the firm (V), which is then employed in equation (6) as a substitute for actual initial firm value. Consistent with the agency hypothesis, Ritter finds that the coefficient on value, b_1 (equation (6)), is smaller when the two stage procedure is used. Using our data, b_1 became smaller only when the two stage procedure was used for the subsample of small companies (See Table 6, Rows 3 and 8), providing partial support for the agency hypothesis. This result is intuitively appealing, since larger firms have better developed internal control systems to deter the consumption of excessive perquisites.[17]

In the following section, an alternative valuation formula is estimated using the TSE data set. This specification examines a number of variables that have recently been advanced regarding the valuation of IPO's.

5. Alternative Empirical Formulation And Empirical Results

The relationship between underwriting fees and various issue characteristics is first examined. According to Hughes (1986), the underwriter is compensated for investigation costs and the present value of the expected penalty in the event that the entrepreneur's disclosures are later determined to be false. Thus, one would expect to find some relationship between underwriting fees and issue characteristics. We have selected the number of years of historical financial

TABLE 5. Test of the Wealth Effect Hypothesis - Ritter (1984)[Ψ]

$$V_j = a_0 + a_1\alpha_j + a_2E_j + a_3I_j + u_j$$

Sample	Estimation Method	$\times 10^7$ a_0	$\times 10^7$ a_1	a_2	a_3	R^2
(1) Ritter	WLS	-4.77 (1.05)*	6.27 (1.46)*	14.99 (.28)*	2.59 (.18)*	.91
(2) Ritter	2SWLS	-19.68 (7.98)*	27.98 (11.51)*	11.39 (1.80)*	2.54 (.18)*	.91
(3) TSE	OLS'	.17 (.14)	-.23 (.19)	0.58×10^{-3} (1.92×10^{-3})	-4.37 (3.80)	.08
(4) TSE	2SOLS'	.11 (.09)	-.16 (.13)	-0.01 (.01)	-.96 (1.44)	.05
(5) TSE Large	OLS'	.50 (.41)	-.65 (.53)	-0.46×10^{-2} ($.53 \times 10^{-2}$)	19.35 (19.94)	.23
(6) TSE Large	2SOLS'	1.77 (.19)*	-2.57 (.28)*	-0.48×10^{-2} ($.14 \times 10^{-2}$)	-2.09 (4.01)	.90
(7) TSE Small	OLS'	.04 (.03)	-.05 (.05)	0.33×10^{-2} ($.13 \times 10^{-2}$)*	-.88 (1.11)	.09
(8) TSE Small	2SOLS'	.32 (.03)*	-.55 (.06)*	1.98×10^{-2} ($.18 \times 10^{-2}$)*	.04 (.11)	.91

Ψ   Standard errors in parentheses.
OLS' Standard errors estimated with White's (1980) heteroskedasticity consistent covariance matrix.
*   Significant at the 5 percent level.

statement data provided in the prospectus as an indicator of investigation costs. Younger firms, which are also smaller, have less data to aid in the valuation process, increasing the complexity of estimating the future cash flows, and thus, a suitable offer price. Underwriting cost as a percentage of total proceeds is also expected to be inversely related to the size of the issue, due to economies of scale in the provision of underwriting services. Further, the net proceeds from the issue may be designated for new investment projects or for refinancing an existing operation. Since the entrepreneur is likely to go through the refinancing process only if it is to his/her benefit, one would expect underwriting fees to be positively related to a reduction in the financial leverage of the company.

TABLE 6. Test of the Agency Hypothesis - Ritter (1984)[ψ]

$$\alpha_j = b_0 + b_1 V_j + b_2 E_j + b_3 \ln SG_j + u_j$$

Sample	Estimation Method	b_0	b_1	b_2	b_3	R^2
(1) Ritter	OLS	.679 (.007)*	1.015×10^{-9} $(.183 \times 10^{-9})$*	-1.763×10^{-9} (3.63×10^{-9})*	.056 (.022)*	.19
(2) Ritter	2SOLS	.680 (.007)*	$-.028 \times 10^{-9}$ $(.406 \times 10^{-9})$	16.737×10^{-9} (7.03×10^{-9})*	.073 (.022)*	.15
(3) TSE	OLS'	.659 (.027)*	$-.201 \times 10^{-6}$ $(.059 \times 10^{-6})$*	$.406 \times 10^{-5}$ $(.267 \times 10^{-5})$	.016 (.072)	.14
(4) TSE	2SOLS'	.674 (.027)*	$.277 \times 10^{-6}$ $(.112 \times 10^{-6})$*	$.315 \times 10^{-5}$ $(.092 \times 10^{-5})$*	-.002 (.02)	.41
(5) TSE large	OLS'	.661 (.035)*	$-.334 \times 10^{-7}$ $(.095 \times 10^{-7})$*	$.108 \times 10^{-9}$ (1.15×10^{-9})	.187 (.15)	.24
(6) TSE large	2SOLS'	.727 (.009)*	$.154 \times 10^{-6}$ $(.006 \times 10^{-6})$*	$.413 \times 10^{-5}$ $(.026 \times 10^{-5})$*	.007 (.026)	.96
(7) TSE small	OLS'	.570 (.039)*	$-.166 \times 10^{-6}$ $(.076 \times 10^{-6})$*	$.371 \times 10^{-8}$ $(.315 \times 10^{-8})$	.066 (.098)	.10
(8) TSE small	2SOLS'	.651 (.034)*	$-.939 \times 10^{-7}$ $(.938 \times 10^{-7})$	$-.331 \times 10^{-4}$ $(.266 \times 10^{-4})$	-.033 (.030)	.07

[ψ]   Standard errors in parentheses.
OLS'   Standard errors estimated with White's (1980)
       heteroskedasticity consistent covariance matrix.
*   Significant at the 5 percent level.

The previous discussion pointed out that one of the main purposes of the paper is to compare and discriminate between "small" and "large" companies. It is impossible, a priori, to discriminate between the two subsamples on a purely economic basis. It is only possible to make positive statements on econometric grounds. We therefore estimate the relationship between underwriting fees and issue characteristics for the two subsamples and the full sample using the following equation;

$$UNDPER_j = \alpha_0 + \alpha_1 \ln TPRO_j + \alpha_2 YRSDAT_j + \alpha_3 DUM_j + u_j \qquad (7)$$

where:

UNDPER$_j$ = the proportion of total proceeds spent on underwriting fees,

1nTPRO$_j$ = the natural log of total proceeds for the jth initial offering,

YRSDAT$_j$ = the number of years of historical financial statement data provided in the jth prospectus,

DUM$_j$ = a dummy variable equal to one if the jth offering involves the retirement of outstanding preferred shares or debt and is equal to zero otherwise, and

u$_j$ = an $N(0, \sigma_u^2)$ distributed disturbance term corresponding to the jth offering.

Table 7 contains the estimated results using the three alternative samples. Since significant heteroskedasticity is present, White's (1980) heteroskedasticity-consistent estimation of the variance-covariance matrix is used in computing standard errors.

The results support the arguments discussed above. In particular, for all samples, underwriting percentage is negatively related to issue size and to data availability, indicating that economies of scale and our proxy for lower investigation costs are significant elements in the fee structure of intermediaries. The coefficient α_1 is statistically significant only for small companies and for the sample as a whole.

In model II, the dependent variable is 1n UNDPRO i.e., the natural log of the dollar proceeds paid for underwriting services. Expressing the dependent variable in log form allows the interpretation of α_1 as the elasticity of underwriting costs with respect to total proceeds. The results are similar for model II, where, as expected, $\alpha_1 < 1$. Further, the elasticity of underwriting costs with respect to total proceeds is negative for both subsamples and is larger for the small firms. That is, the same increase in size has a greater impact on underwriting fees for smaller companies.[18] The refinancing of existing operations turned out to be relatively expensive ($\alpha_3 > 0$). Entrepreneurs electing to substitute new outside equity for outstanding fixed income securities must pay a higher percentage of total proceeds in underwriting fees. These relationships turned out to be significant only for large firms and for the full sample.[19]

Based on the Chow (1960) test, both the large and small firm subsamples obey the same relationship.[20] This implies that although small firms are paying higher underwriting fees (see the rank test in Table 3), the fee structure of intermediaries is based not on firm size, but on other issue characteristics.

Overall, the empirical evidence supports the notion that underwriters charge differential fees on the basis of issue characteristics. One would, therefore, expect investors to utilize this information in valuing new issues. We have included the proportion of total proceeds used to compensate the underwriter in the examination of various signalling mechanisms below. Underwriting fees, entrepreneurial ownership retention, underwriter quality and direct accounting disclosures are simultaneously tested for potential signalling value.

As in previous studies, direct disclosures in the offering prospectus are included in the valuation model to reduce the effect of sample heterogeneity on the signalling variable coefficients. As 29 percent of the new issues are for resource-related firms (mining or oil and gas), the amount of net proceeds designated for exploration and development activities is included as an independent variable. Research and development activities by industrial firms are also captured

TABLE 7. Tests of the Determinants of Underwriting Fees[ψ]

$$UNDPER_j = \alpha_0 + \alpha_1 \ln TPRO_j + \alpha_2 YRSDAT_j + \alpha_3 DUM_j + u_j$$

Model	Sample	α_0	α_1	α_2	α_3	$\overline{R^2}$
I	TOTAL	.093 (10.11)*	-.003 (-2.97)*	-.002 (-3.06)*	.004 (2.31)*	.136
I	LARGE	.082 (7.92)*	-.002 (-1.62)	-.002 (-2.66)*	.004 (1.92)**	.128
I	SMALL	.093 (7.42)*	-.003 (-2.16)*	-.001 (-1.71)**	.004 (1.29)	.093
II	TOTAL	-2.380 (-15.54)*	-.037 (-2.29)*	-.024 (-2.86)*	.070 (2.28)*	.107
II	LARGE	-2.493 (-14.48)*	-.025 (-1.52)	-.026 (-2.34)*	.067 (2.04)*	.099
II	SMALL	-2.388 (11.41)*	-.035 (-1.55)	-.021 (-1.71)**	.070 (1.24)	.060

[ψ]   t-values in parentheses (using white's (1980) heteroskedasticity consistent covariance matrix).
*   Significant at the 5 percent level.
** Significant at the 10 percent level.

by this variable. This specification is similar to Beatty and Ritter (1986), where the number of uses of issue proceeds designated in the prospectus is included as a proxy for the issue's ex-ante uncertainty. The size of the sample firms prior to the initial public offering is also explicitly considered through the inclusion of a dummy variable set equal to one for the "large" firms and to zero for the "small" firms. Various specifications of the following formula are employed to examine the empirical validity of the above hypotheses:

$$\ln V_j = \gamma_0 + \gamma_1 \alpha_j + \gamma_2 UWQ_j + \gamma_3 UNDPER_j + \gamma_4 \ln EXPDEV_j + \gamma_5 SIZE_j + u_j \quad (8)$$

where:

UWQ_j = a dummy variable equal to one for high quality or "prestigious" underwriters and to zero otherwise,

$\ln EXPDEV_j$ = the natural log of issue proceeds designated

for exploration and development activities,
and

SIZE$_j$ = a dummy variable equal to one for "large" firms and to zero otherwise.

Each of the suggested signalling mechanisms has the predicted relationship with initial firm value (see Table 8) and most are significant at the 10 percent level. The LP ownership retention signal has the correct sign, but in our sample it is never significant. Given our data set, we could not support the hypothesis that the level of shareholdings retained by the entrepreneur reveals his private information and thus increases issue value. In models (2) to (4), various market prices (first day closing and first week closing) are used instead of the subscription price.

The results are not sensitive to alternative specifications of initial firm value. The results support the hypothesis that underwriter quality and service fees are related to the pricing of initial public offerings. Initial firm value is positively related to underwriter quality[21] and negatively related to underwriting fees. Further, direct disclosure of the use of issue proceeds is a significant explanatory variable in the valuation process. Given our definition of this variable, this finding may represent a correction for cross-sectional variations in ex ante uncertainty regarding future cash flows, which is a function of the riskiness of proposed investments. The magnitude of assets in place is a direct accounting disclosure that proved to be relevant to the valuation process.[22] As expected, larger firms achieve, ceteris paribus, higher value in the market.

TABLE 8. Test of Signalling Hypotheses[ψ]

$$\ln V_j = \gamma_0 + \gamma_1 \alpha_j + \gamma_2 UWQ_j + \gamma_3 UNDPER_j + \gamma_4 \ln EXPDEV_j + \gamma_5 SIZE_j + u_j$$

	Dependent Variable	γ_0	γ_1	γ_2	γ_3	γ_4	γ_5	$\overline{R^2}$
(1)	Subscription Price $ Current	10.101 (11.97)*	-.056 (-.36)	.683 (2.88)*	-16.041 (-1.37)	.068 (2.93)*	.672 (3.47)*	.194
(2)	Subscription Price $ Constant	10.069 (11.44)*	-.133 (-.83)	.673 (2.96)*	-7.280 (-.54)	.038 (1.50)	.486 (2.18)*	.043
(3)	Initial Market Price $ Current	9.850 (12.57)*	-.063 (-.41)	.746 (3.31)*	-11.815 (-1.04)	.054 (2.48)*	.700 (3.78)*	.188
(4)	Initial Market Price $ Constant	9.814 (11.37)*	-.140 (-.86)	.736 (3.30)*	-3.033 (-.22)	.024 (1.00)	.515 (2.32)*	.043

ψ   n = 115, t-values in parentheses (using White's (1980) heteroskedasticity consistent covariance matrix).

*   significant at the 5 percent level.

6. Summary

This investigation of the initial offering process in the Canadian institutional setting is the first to explicitly distinguish between large and small issuing firms. Empirical specifications employed in previous studies are first re-estimated and it is shown that after adjusting for heteroskedasticity, most of the results can not be replicated. In particular, we do not detect a significant coefficient for the entrepreneurial ownership retention signal in any specification, although it is of the predicted sign. This result holds both for the total sample and for the large and small firm subsamples. As in the original study by Ritter (1984), the wealth effect hypothesis is not supported (although for different reasons) and the agency hypothesis appears to hold only for the subsample of small firms. We also examine whether there are size related biases in the capital acquisition process. Although larger firms pay a smaller portion of total issue proceeds in underwriting fees, this is explained by issue characteristics other than firm size. Key variables include the size of the issue, the nature of the offering and the availability of historical financial data in the offering prospectus. In short, large and small issuing firms appear to be paying fees based on the same underlying schedule. The proportion of total proceeds paid to underwriters is then included as an additional signal in the valuation model. An inverse relationship is detected between initial firm value and underwriting fees, supporting the notion that the underwriting fee schedule has information content. As in earlier studies, issuing firms employing a high quality or 'prestigious' underwriter have higher initial value. For all definitions of initial value employed (market vs. subscription prices), and after controlling for other information available to investors, initial value is found to be significantly higher for firms with a high book value of assets prior to the offering.

Endnotes

1. For theoretical models of various signalling mechanisms see: Leland and Pyle (1977), and Hughes (1986) on entrepreneurial ownership retention; Ross (1977) on financial leverage; Bhattacharya (1979) on dividend policy, Bhattacharya and Ritter (1983), and Hughes (1986) on direct disclosures; Titman and Trueman (1986), Beatty (1986, 1987), Feltham and Hughes (1987), and Tinic (1988) on auditor or investment banker quality. The choice of accounting policies, disclosure practices and measurement methods may also provide an indication of managements' future actions and interventions (see, for example, Watts and Zimmerman, 1986; Thornton, 1986).

2. A significant proportion of the small firm effect is observed during the month of January (see, for example, Blume and Stambaugh, 1983). It is partially explained by the tax loss selling hypothesis (Reinganum, 1983).

3. One should note, however, that the decision by the entrepreneur on how much to retain is not motivated solely by portfolio considerations. An important factor is the maintenance of control. (The authors would like to thank Lemma Senbet for bringing this point to their attention.)

4. They also examine the Bhattacharya (1979) and Heinkel (1978) models in which dividend policy serves as a signal of firm value. The hypothesis that higher value firms pay higher dividends was rejected.

5. The Downes and Heinkel (1982) sample was limited to firms with at least three years of operating data and initial price-earnings ratios below 40 (p.4).

6. Ritter (1984) sheds some doubt on the empirical validity of the LP signal. He tests three potential explanations for the positive empirical relation between firm value and insider holdings and finds that of three alternatives, the LP, wealth, and agency hypotheses, the latter fares the best.

7. Their model "is also applicable to the choice of investment banker quality or more generally, to the choice of any outsider who can provide information about the firm" (p. 160).

8. Beatty (1987) and Simunic and Stein (1987) provide evidence that larger and less risky initial public offering clients tend to hire Big Eight CPA firms.

9. The Mann-Whitney U test (Wilcoxon Sum of the Ranks test) is employed here.

10. While the Titman and Trueman (1986) model suggests that quality be measured along a continuum, they recognize that the practical alternative is to partition the data into two quality levels and to treat quality as a dummy variable for the purpose of empirical tests.

11. As was evident in the aftermath of the recent BP issue, underwriting firms can assume significant financial risk relative to their net worth, even when individual underwriters handle only a small portion of the issue.

12. Replacing the offer price with the price in the immediate after market does not alter the results. Similar robustness to alternative measurements of initial value were also obtained by Downes and Heinkel (1982) (see their footnote 4, p. 6).

13. Both of the selected weighting variables also eliminate any problems that might arise due to cross sectional variations in scale when the full sample is employed.

14. We also experimented with first week closing prices. Again, no significant change in results was obtained.

15. For the full sample, the coefficient on the LP signal using this specification is -0.48975×10^{-4}, with a standard error of 0.40528×10^{-4}. The adjusted R^2 is $-.0049$.

16. In The Chow (1960) test, the model is estimated once using just the subsample of small firms and then using the pooled (large and small firm) data. The null hypothesis is that the additional observations obey the same relationship as those in the smaller sample. Conducting this test on equation (5) results in an $F(52,112)$ statistic of 777.7. Thus, the null hypothesis that small and large firm subsamples obey the same relationship is rejected at conventional levels of significance.

17. The Chow (1960) test for structural differences indicates no difference for the two subsamples, as the $F(52,112)$ statistic had a value of only .105.

18. This might indicate a declining average cost curve.

19. The TSE requires industrial firms to disclose three years of historical financial data in the prospectus of an initial public offering. To examine whether the YRSDAT variable captures an industry effect, we re-estimated equation (7) adding a dummy variable set to one for industrial firms. The sign and significance of the parameter for YRSDAT were unaffected.

20. $F(52,112) = .968$.

21. A cross tabulation of the two dummy variables representing firm size (SIZE) and underwriter quality (UWQ) has a chi-square of only 1.682, indicating that there is no statistically significant relationship between these variables that could confound the reported results.

22. Unlike previous studies (Downes and Heinkel, 1982) we found no evidence of significant relationships between initial firm value and the historical sales revenue or the profit margin from existing operations.

References

Barry, C.B. and Brown, S.J. (1984) 'Differential Information and the Small Firm Effect', Journal of Financial Economics, 283-294.

Barry, C.B. and Brown S.J. (December 1985) 'Differential Information and Security Market Equilibrium', Journal of Financial and Quantitative Analysis, 407-434.

Beatty, R.P. (February 1986) 'The Initial Public Offerings Market for Auditing Services', Working Paper, The Wharton School, University of Pennsylvania.

Beatty, R.P. (May 1987) 'Auditor Reputation and the Pricing of Initial Public Offerings', Working Paper, The Wharton School, University of Pennsylvania.

Beatty, R.P. and Ritter, J.R. (June 1986) 'Investment Banking Reputations and the Underpricing of Initial Public Offerings', Journal of Financial Economics, 213-232.

Bhattacharya, S. (Spring 1979) 'Imperfect Information, Dividend Policy, and the Bird in the Hand Fallacy', Bell Journal of Economics, 259-270.

Bhattacharya, S. and Ritter J.R. (July 1983) 'Innovation and Communication: Signalling with Partial Disclosure', Review of Economic Studies, 331-346.

Blume, M.E. and Staumbaugh, R.F. (June 1983) 'Biases in Computed Returns, An Application to the Size Effect', Journal of Financial Economics, 387-404.

Chow, G.C. (July 1960) 'Tests of Equality Between Sets of Coefficients in Two Linear Regressions', Econometrica, 591-605.

Downes, D.H. and Heinkel R. (March 1982) 'Signalling and the Valuation of Unseasoned New Issues', Journal of Finance, 1-10.

Feltham, G.A. and Hughes, J.S. (January 1987) 'The Role of Audits and Audit Quality in Valuing New Issues', Working Paper, Faculty of Commerce and Business Administration, University of British Columbia.

Heinkel, R. (1978) Dividend Policy as a Signal of Firm Value, Four Essays on Financial Markets with Imperfect Information, Ph.D. Dissertation, University of California, Berkeley.

Hughes, J.S. (Spring 1989) Discussion of "The Valuation of Initial Public Offerings", Contemporary Accounting Research, 519-525.

Hughes, P. (June 1986) 'Signalling by Direct Disclosure', Journal of Accounting and Economics, 119-142.

Ibbotson, R.G. (June 1985) 'Price Performance of Common Stock New Issues', Journal of Financial Economics, 235-272.

18

Klein, R.W. and Bawa, V. S. (1977) 'The Effect of Limited Information and Estimation Risk on Optimal Portfolio Diversification', Journal of Financial Economics, 89-111.

Lakonishok, J. and Smidt, S. (forthcoming 1989) 'Are Seasonal Anomalies Real?', Review of Financial Studies.

Krinsky, I. and Rotenberg, W. (Spring 1989) 'The Valuation of Initial Public Offerings', Contemporary Accounting Research, 501-515.

Leland, H.E. and Pyle, D.H. (May 1977) 'Information Asymmetries, Financial Structure and Financial Intermediation', Journal of Finance, 371-387.

Logue, D.E. (January 1973) 'On the Pricing of Unseasoned Equity Offerings: 1965-1969', Journal of Financial and Quantitative Analysis, 91-104.

Reinganum, M.R. (June 1983) 'The Anomolous Stock Market Behavior of Small Firms in January: Empirical Tests for Tax-Loss Selling Effects', Journal of Financial Economics, 89-104.

Ritter, J.R. (September 1984) 'Signalling and the Valuation of Unseasoned New Issues: A Comment', Journal of Finance, 1231-1237.

Roll, R. (September 1981) 'A Possible Explanation of the Small Firm Effect', Journal of Finance, 879-887.

Ross, S. (Spring 1977) 'The Determination of Financial Structure: The Incentive -Signalling Approach', Bell Journal of Economics, 23-40.

Simunic, D. and Stein, M. (1987) Product Differentiation in Auditing: A Study of Auditor Choice in the Market for New Issues (Certified General Accountant's Research Foundation).

Thornton, D.B. (Fall 1986) 'Current Cost Disclosers and Nondisclosers: Canadian Evidence', Contemporary Accounting Research, 1-34.

Tinic, S.M. (September 1988) 'Anatomy of Initial Public Offerings of Common Stock', Journal of Finance, 789-822.

Titman, S. and Trueman, B. (June 1986) 'Information Quality and the Valuation of New Issues', Journal of Accounting and Economics, 159-172.

Watts, R.L. and Zimmerman, S.L. (1986) Positive Accounting Theory (Prentice-Hall, Englewood Cliffs, N.J.).

White, H. (1980) 'A Heteroskedasticity - Consistent Covariance Matrix Estimator and a Direct Test for Heteroskedasticity', Econometrica, 817-838.

PRICING MINORITY DISCOUNTS
IN CLOSELY-HELD CORPORATIONS

JEROME S. OSTERYOUNG
College of Business
Florida State University
Tallahassee, FL 32306

DONALD A. NAST
College of Business
Florida State University
Tallahassee, FL 32306

WILLIAM H. WELLS
College of Business
Florida State University
Tallahassee, FL 32306

ABSTRACT. The purpose of this research is to investigate the pricing of minority discounts in small private firms. An option pricing model is developed that allows the specification of the minority discounts. With this model the computation of the minority discount can be computed without having the option actually exist.

1. Introduction

The valuation of closely-held corporations presents several problems.[1] In the absence of market forces that assure us that widely traded assets are fairly priced, closely-held corporations and their shares must be assessed on a firm by firm basis. In addition, these corporations pose a unique problem. Unlike securities of widely traded corporations, shares of closely-held firms are not necessarily homogeneous. Shares owned by minority investors are commonly considered to be of less value than those of majority shareholders (or, more accurately, controlling shareholders). Frequently, this phenomenon is described as "the sum of the parts do not equal the value of the whole." Minority shares are typically priced at a discount from their pro rata value due to lack of marketability or lack of control.

The valuation of minority shares has received attention primarily in our courts. The Internal Revenue Service (IRS) and private parties are frequently at odds in valuing minority interests for tax purposes. Estate and gift taxes are based on asset value so the two parties have polar objectives in placing value on the assets in question. Therefore, it is usually left to the courts

19

R. Yazdipour (ed.), Advances in Small Business Finance, 19–28.
© 1991 *Kluwer Academic Publishers. Printed in the Netherlands.*

to decide what value is appropriate. Unfortunately, very little financial theory has been applied to these cases. Instead, rules of thumb are frequently tossed about and previous court decisions cited as support for various discount rates.[2]

The purpose of this paper is to apply finance theory to the valuation of minority shares. It will become apparent that lack of control is the only factor that should enter the discounting process. We show that the risk of diversion of value from minority owners to controlling owners can be reduced or eliminated. Further, protection can be identified and priced so that minority shares are valued at their pro rata share of the corporation's value.

Section two reviews traditional minority discounting literature including court case summaries and empirical evidence. The third section explores the relationship between minority discounts and control premiums.

Section four introduces the application of finance theory to the minority discount problem. An option pricing solution to minority discounts is presented. The last section provides a summary and implications for future minority valuation cases.

2. The Traditional Approach

The majority of literature related to minority share valuation has been legal analysis. The reason is simple if not justifiable. Because shares of closely held firms are exchanged infrequently, valuation is rarely needed. Most valuations arise as a result of gift or estate transfers. Share value must be determined so that taxes may be assessed. It takes little imagination to perceive the possible problems that may arise.

The IRS and private parties obviously have conflicting motives in arriving at share values. Private parties, through appraisers, argue that steep discounts from pro rata values should apply. Naturally, the IRS holds the position that little or no discount is applicable. The result is that the dispute is left to the courts to resolve.

The judges of these trials rely on the evidence produced by expert witnesses for both parties. It must surely perplex the courts when the IRS suggests a minority discount of 10% and the private party's witness presents evidence supporting a discount of 70%. No wonder the courts have allowed a wide range of discounts for minority shares. Frequently, the courts arrive at discounts independently and do not use the discount from either witness.[3]

What is of concern is that previous court rulings are often presented as evidence to support claims of discounts. This practice only serves to perpetuate myths and the 'rule of thumb' approach that dominates this problem. The decision of whether or not a discount is applicable may be a legal question, but the derivation of an appropriate discount should be based on sound finance theory. Horsman (1987) rejects the use of previous court decisions to support specific discounts. Each case should be decided on its own based on the relevant information.

Because the intent of this paper is to focus on financial theory as it applies to valuing minority shares, specific court cases will not be reviewed.[4] However, it may be helpful to examine the comments of legal scholars. Their views will, hopefully, provide some insights that will lead us to a rational solution to the discounting puzzle. Several empirical studies that attempt to determine appropriate discount rates are examined (Coolidge 1975, Emory 1985, Maher 1976, Moroney 1973).

Krishna (1987) represents the contingency that cannot isolate those factors that apply to all shares of a closely-held corporation from those that apply only to minority shares. According to this faction, minority discounts may be justified for any and all of the following reasons:

1. lack of marketability;
2. restrictions on transfer;
3. small corporations business risk;
4. dependence of business on a key person;
5. inability of minority to control dividend policy; or
6. lack of influence by minority on management policies.

This list illustrates the confusion prevalent in valuing closely-held firms and establishing a basis for a minority discount. Matters are simplified if the first three factors are lumped together and called lack of marketability (or illiquidity). The last two factors are control. Factor four might be included with lack of marketability or, in some cases, control.

Clearly, marketability factors influence the value of the entire corporation. These risk elements are implicitly built into the price of the firm as an operating unit. If a discount for lack of marketability is explicitly applied to minority shares, double discounting occurs.

Emory (1985) examines initial public offerings and private transactions that occurred within five months of the offering. Emory finds that the private transactions took place at discounts ranging from 4 percent to 66 percent. The average discount is 60 percent. It is assumed that the private transactions occur at fair market value at the time of the transactions. Several weaknesses are apparent in this study.

Top level managers frequently receive stocks as bonuses. In addition, options to purchase shares at favorable prices are sold to managers. It is inconceivable that the management of the subject corporations were not aware that their firms planned to go public. With this in mind, it is more than reasonable that the transactions did not take place at fair market value. We suggest that the privately transferred securities are options based on expected offering prices. The proof of this hypothesis is beyond the scope of this paper.

Moroney (1973) goes to great lengths to support minority discounts up to 90%. The study examines purchase prices of restricted securities held by ten investment corporations.[5] The purchase prices are compared to the market price of freely traded securities and the difference in prices is assumed to be a discount for lack of marketability. An analogy is made between these securities and minority shares of closely-held corporations. Even though discounts range from 3% to 90%, Moroney concentrates his discussion on the upper values. In addition, it is suggested that minority shares of closely-held firms should have higher discounts, because the restricted securities will become marketable within two years.

> Moroney states:
> Some appraisers have, for years, had a strong gut feeling that they should use far greater discounts for nonmarketability than the courts had allowed. From now on, those appraisers need not stop at 35 percent merely because it's perhaps the largest discount clearly approved in a court decision. Appraisers can now cite a number of known arm's length transactions in which the discount ranged up to 90 percent.

This statement illustrates the weaknesses inherent with the traditional methods of determining minority discounts. First, 'gut feelings' rather than financial theory tend to provide appraisers with their basis for valuation. Secondly, relying on the 35 percent rule of thumb figure from previous court cases creates a credibility problem. An expert witness is not required if testimony consists of citing previous legal decisions. Finally, focusing on the extreme high range of values taken from a class of securities that may have little, if anything, in common with minority shares removes any semblance of objectivity from the study.

Coolidge (1975) and Maher (1976) also examine restricted securities prices in an effort to establish evidence of, and guidelines for, discounts for lack of marketability. Both studies found that discounts averaged approximately 35% of market value. However, the two studies differ on the application of the discount. Coolidge applies the entire 35 percent discount to minority shares. Coolidge suggests that letter stocks are analogous to minority interests in closely-held corporations due to their illiquidity. Letter stocks are restricted from trading on the market and the minority shares lack control over the corporation. Coolidge makes the assumption that lack of control causes illiquidity. But we know that closely-held businesses are inherently illiquid. It is the underlying lack of marketability of the corporation that is reflected in all shares, majority blocks as well as minority holdings.

Maher recognizes that the lack of marketability discount derived from the restricted securities analysis should be applied to all shares of the closely-held corporation. Any discounts due to lack of control must be calculated independently. This is not a trivial point. Illiquidity applies to the corporation as a whole and, therefore, every individual share of the corporation. Discounts for lack of control are unique to the minority shares if they exist at all.

3. The Relationship Between Controlling and Minority Shares

3.1. THE EXISTENCE OF CONTROLLING BLOCKS

Consider the implications of the existence of a minority discount based on a lack of control. For control to be a relevant factor, we must assume that those in control have an advantage over those without control (minority owners). Further, those in control must be able to divert wealth (share value) to themselves at the expense of minority owners.

Hall (1982) provides an important clue that is often over-looked. Discounting minority shares suggests that majority shares should be valued at a premium. That is, value is diverted from minority to majority (controlling) owners. The amount of the minority discount is limited by the potential diversion of value from minority owners to majority owners. The probability that those in control will actually take actions that benefit themselves at the expense of the minority owners must be considered. If it can be determined that the probability is very small or zero, there should be little or no discount for lack of control.

Hall recognizes that the minority discount does not vary with the size of the minority block, but is constant for a given corporation. Without this assumption, one might incorrectly conclude that the minority discount (control premium) is a function of the size of the minority (majority) block. The relationship between discounts and premiums is illustrated where:

M is the pro rata value of the minority block
C is the pro rata value of the majority block
P is the pro rata value of each share
X is the value of the firm
m is the number of minority shares
c is the number of majority shares
α is the minority discount

β is the majority premium and,

$$M + C = X$$

After adjusting for the discount and premium, we have:

$$M * (1 - \alpha) + C * (1 + \beta) = X$$

The distribution of value changes, but total firm value remains constant. It is also clear that:

$$\alpha * M = \beta * C$$

The value of the discount equals the value of the premium. The controlling block can only gain what it diverts from the minority block.[6]

Solving for b, we have:

$$\beta = \frac{\alpha * M}{C}$$

where,

$$M = P * m$$
$$C = P * c$$

substituting yields,

$$\beta = \frac{\alpha * m}{c}$$

From this equality, we see that the controlling premium varies proportionately with the size of the minority block. This does not imply that large minority blocks are more vulnerable to diversion, but that there is a larger aggregate of wealth available to divert.

The value of α is derived from examining the characteristics of individual corporations. Hall points out that α may vary for a specific corporation depending on such factors as the articles of incorporation. For example, supermajority requirements for some decisions may cause α to have one value if the controlling block is less than a supermajority and a higher value if a supermajority block is held.

The converse of deriving the control premium from a minority discount is that the presence of a control premium implies the existence of a minority discount. If a controlling interest does not exist, then there is no justification for a minority discount. This rationale has been consistently overlooked by the courts and commentators.

3.2. PROTECTING MINORITY INTERESTS

Minority shareholders are not without some protection from unscrupulous controlling parties. Houlihan (1981), O'Neal (1987) and Hall discuss the legal rights of minority interests. Along with common law fiduciary duty and state corporation statutes, corporate charters may contain provisions that reduce the probability that minority interests will be victimized.

Houlihan reviews several cases where the courts support the theory that majority shareholders owe a fiduciary duty to minority shareholders. The relationship between majority and minority interests is analogous to that of director and minority shareholder. The director is charged with the responsibility of acting in the best interest of the corporation and its shareholders.

O'Neal suggests that fiduciary duty provides minority shareholders with considerable protection. Contrary to other majority infractions, such as fraud, the fiduciary has the burden of justifying his conduct. The elements of fraud are numerous and, frequently, difficult to prove. Houlihan's review of cases based on breach of fiduciary duty confirms that controlling parties are accountable to all shareholders, including minority interests.

O'Neal offers several methods for preventing controlling parties from diverting wealth from minority shareholders. These precautions include shareholders' agreements, long-term employment contracts and charter provisions requiring supermajority votes for important actions.

In spite of the legal protection available to minority shareholders, substantial discounts are routinely applied to minority shares. Discounts are acknowledged by the courts even in cases where no evidence of a controlling entity exists.

Several possibilities may account for this phenomenon. Foremost among the possible explanations is the cost associated with the development and enforcement of restrictive agreements. Minority shareholders must seek independent legal counsel to assure themselves that their interests are adequately protected. This is an expense that may be waived by investors, especially when dealing with family and personal relations.

The expenses associated with seeking legal recourse for wrongful activities by controlling owners is expensive and time consuming. Minority owners may be reluctant to pursue retribution when their share values are relatively small. The cost may outweigh any possible gain. If controlling parties are aware of minority shareholders' reluctance to enforce state statutes and corporate articles, they may act as if such restrictions do not exist. Therefore, minority shares continue to be discounted.

4. Pricing the Minority Discount

Contrary to the evidence indicating minority discounts should not exist, they are regularly observed. We have suggested reasons for their presence. But the explanations for their existence leaves unanswered the question of magnitude. In this section, we propose a method for deriving the correct discount for individual corporations.

Jensen and Meckling (1976) address the issue of raising external capital when agency problems exist. Incentive conflicts occur as owner-managers (controlling parties) make decisions that enhance their wealth at the expense of other investors. Jensen and Meckling find that costs are incurred when funds are sought from outsiders. Owner-managers may consume perks to the extent that share values are reduced unnecessarily. These costs are analogous to the diversion of value from minority shares to controlling shares.

Haugen and Senbet (1981) provide a solution to the agency problem with options. Through the use of options, controlling parties may be forced to take actions that are in the best interest of minority shareholders. By taking these actions, the controlling parties are forced to limit the consumption of perks and other activities that reduce the value of minority shares.

In their solution to the agency problem, Haugen and Senbet attach an option to the contract for funds. In our application of this solution, minority shareholders receive a put option from the controlling party as part of the equity issuance. The exercise price of the option is the expected pro rata share value of the firm at the end of a specified time period. Should the value of minority shares fall below the expected end of period value, minority owners may exercise their options.

If we can show that diversion of minority share value can be prevented through the use of contingency claims, we can also price the risk of diversion. The price of a put option that limits the risk of minority shareholders represents the reduction in minority share value due to lack of control. The price of the option is the value of the discount.

Two simplifying assumptions are made by Haugen and Senbet. Investors are risk neutral so the expected return on all assets is the risk-free rate. Secondly, the terminal value of the firm is uniformly distributed over the interval [V1, V2], and V2 is the limiting value. The value of the European put is specified as:

$$V_p = \phi^{-1} * \left(\frac{1}{R}\right) \int_{V_1}^{E_p} (E_p - X)\, dx = \frac{(E_p - V_1)^2}{2\phi R}$$

where,
ϕ is the risk-free rate of interest
X is a variable of integration for the terminal value of the firm
$R = V_2 - V_1$
$1/R$ is the density function for the uniform distribution
E_p is the exercise price

When the exercise price lies outside the interval [V1, V2], the value of the put option becomes:

$$Vp = 0 \qquad \text{if } E_p < V_1$$
$$Vp = \phi^{-1} * E_p - V \quad \text{if } E_p > V_2$$

where the current value of the firm is:

$$V = \phi^{-1} * \frac{(V_1 + V_2)}{2}$$

The value of the put option in terms of V is:

$$V_p = \frac{(E_p + R/2 - \phi V)^2}{(2\phi R)}$$

Haugen and Senbet's model allows us to place a price on protecting minority share value. It is not required that the option actually exists, but that the theoretical option can be priced. From this model, the price of a put option is the upper limit for the value of a minority discount. Therefore, the fair value of a minority share must fall between the pro rata value and the pro rata value less the price of the option.

Any assessed value below the lower boundary is based on an excessive discount. Prices above the lower boundary may be justified by shareholder agreements or recognition of adequate legislative protection.

5. Conclusion

The question of minority discount has burdened our courts for many years. The courts may continue to decide when and where minority discounts are appropriate, but the value of the discount should be determined by financial theory and analysis. It is unconscionable that discounts are derived as they are. Reliance on previous court rulings may be appropriate for legal decisions, but not for questions of firm value.

When minority shareholders take sufficient precautions, the value of their shares can be protected. The most efficient means of protection is through well-written shareholder agreements. Supermajority vote requirements are particularly helpful to minority interests. State laws may offer protection and relief from adverse actions by controlling parties. Common laws against such acts as fraud and state statutes protecting the rights of minority shareholders discourage controlling parties from diverting value from minority interests.

In the presence of these protective elements, minority discounts are continuously called for. This indicates that the costs associated with creating and/or enforcing the laws are prohibitive. Haugen and Senbet offer a model that allows us to protect minority share value and derive the cost of protection.

For our purposes, the pricing of protection is relevant. Using the Haugen and Senbet solution we can determine the magnitude of the minority discount for individual corporations. It is no longer necessary or excusable to depend on rules of thumb or misspecified empirics in pricing minority discounts.

Endnotes

1. For our purpose, we can define closely-held corporations as having concentrated own ership and such few trades that the transaction does not provide a reliable indicator of fair market value (Joyce 1981).

2. Charles W. Ward and Virginia P. Ward vs Commissioner, 87 T.C. 78, CCH Dec. 43,178 (1986).

3. Dant (1975) provides a summary of relevant cases with the discounts suggested by the experts and the discounts allowed by the judges.

4. For frequently cited cases see Moroney (1973) and Dant (1975). Hall (1982) provides analyses of several relevant cases.

5. Solberg (1979) provides a thorough description of the characteristics of restricted secu rities.

6. Conversely, the loss of value to minority owners is limited to the amount that can be diverted to the majority owners.

References

Coolidge, H. Calvin (Spring 1975) 'Fixing value of minority interest in abusiness; actual sales suggest discount as high as 70%', Estate Planning.

Dant Jr., Thomas W. (August 1975) 'Courts increasing amount of discount for aminority interest in a business', Journal of Taxation.

Emory, John D. (September 1985) 'The Value of Marketability as Illustrated in Initial Public Offerings of Common Stock', Business Valuation News.

Hall, Thomas D. (Winter 1982) 'Valuing Closely Held Stock: Control Premiums and Minority Discounts', Emory Law Journal.

Haugen, Robert A. and Senbet, Lemma W. (June 1981) 'Resolving the Agency Problem of External Capital through Options', Journal of Finance.

Horsman, Steven E. (July 1987) 'Minority Discounts on Gifts Among Family Members', Trusts & Estates.

Houlihan, A. Patricia (Spring 1980 - 1981) 'Corporate Law - Majority Shareholders of a Corporation Owe a Fiduciary Duty to Minority Shareholders of Recovery Distinct from Fraud', Drake Law Review.

Jensen, M. C. and Meckling, W. H. (October 1976) 'Theory of the Firm: Managerial Behavior, Agency Costs and Ownership Structure', Journal of Financial Economics.

Krishna, Vern (September 1987) 'Determining the 'Fair Value' of Corporate Shares', Canadian Business Law Journal.

Maher, J. Michael (September 1976) 'Discounts for Lack of Marketability for Closely Held Business Interests', Taxes - The Tax Magazine.

Moroney, Robert E. (March 1973) 'Most Courts Overvalue Closely Held Stocks', Taxes - The Tax Magazine.

O'Neal, F. Hodge (Winter/Spring 1986) 'Oppression of Minority Shareholders: Protecting Minority Rights', Cleveland State Law Review.

Solberg, Thomas A. (September 1979) 'Valuing restricted securities: what factors do the courts and the service look for?', Journal of Taxation..

ASSET-BASED FINANCING AND THE DETERMINANTS OF CAPITAL STRUCTURE IN THE SMALL FIRM

RICHARD L. CONSTAND
College of Business Administration
University of Hawaii at Manoa
Honolulu, HI 96822

JEROME S. OSTERYOUNG
College of Business
Florida State University
Tallahassee, FL 32306

DONALD A. NAST
College of Business
Florida State University
Tallahassee, FL 32306

ABSTRACT. Small firm debt financing differs from large firm debt financing. Most studies of the determinants of capital structure examine large, publicly owned and traded firms that rely on the issuance of bonds for their debt financing. This study examines the determinants of capital structure in small, privately owned firms that rely heavily on secured commercial loans (Asset-Based Loans) for their debt financing. The results of the empirical analysis indicate that a small firm's asset structure is the most important determinant of the use of debt financing.

1. Introduction

Small and mid-sized firms play a major role in the United States (U.S.) economy. Of the three million corporations in the U.S., over 97 percent are classified as small businesses by the Small Business Administration. These firms have distinctive characteristics which separate them from very large, publicly traded corporations which usually serve as a basis for theoretical and empirical work in Finance. One of the major characteristic differences between large firms and smaller firms is associated with the methods of debt financing used. Smaller firms rely heavily on secured commercial loans obtained from banks for their debt financing needs while larger firms often issue unsecured bonds in the financial markets. It is the purpose of this study to examine the capital structures associated with the methods of secured debt financing used by small firms.

29

R. Yazdipour (ed.), Advances in Small Business Finance, 29–45.
© 1991 *Kluwer Academic Publishers. Printed in the Netherlands.*

2. Secured Debt Financing

One of the most common types of secured financing arrangements used by small and mid-sized firms is the secured revolving loan (revolving Asset-Based Loan or revolving ABL) which is collateralized by accounts receivable accounts and inventory. This type of loan is referred to as a revolving loan because loan disbursements and repayments are made on a daily basis. The maximum amount of funds that the lender is willing to make available to the borrower on any specific day is determined by applying an agreed upon advance rate to the balances of the eligible collateralized accounts. For collateralized inventory, advance rates usually range from 30% to 50% but may be as high as 80%. For receivables, advance rates usually may range from as high as 70% to 90% of acceptable accounts. As the balances of the accounts fluctuate, the amount of the funds the lender is willing to lend (or advance) against the collateral fluctuates as well. The ABL process is discussed extensively in practitioners' publications but has been virtually ignored as a research topic.[1]

Smaller firms also use secured debt financing to fund investments in fixed assets. In most cases medium term and long term assets are purchased with the proceeds of equipment loan notes and mortgage loans. The loans are amortized over the useful lives of the assets so at any point in time the outstanding loan balance reflects the net asset value. These loans are often referred to as ABL's as well.

3. Theoretical Research

Recent theoretical work has contained arguments for the existence of an optimal capital structure at less than 100% debt financing due to the balancing of various agency costs against the tax related benefits of debt financing.[2] Unfortunately, this research often ignores methods of secured debt financing that smaller firms utilize as their major source of capital. Scott (1977, 1979) develops a theoretical model which specifically includes the existence of secured debt in the firm's capital structure. The characteristics of the secured financing appearing in the Scott model closely parallel the characteristics of modern ABL arrangements. There is a direct relationship between the assets available for use as collateral and the use of debt financing.

4. Empirical Research

In addition to the theoretical work, there exists extensive empirical research which attempts to identify the determinants of a corporate capital structure using real world data. Some authors, such as Baxter and Cragg (1970), Martin and Scott (1974), Taub (1975), and Marsh (1982), empirically model the choice between the issuance of equity or debt and test the predictive ability of their models. Most authors, however, focus their attention on identifying the determinants of capital structure.

A number of different factors have been identified as possible determinants of capital structure. Many authors, including Schwarz and Aronson (1967), Gupta (1969), Scott (1972), Schmidt (1976), Scott and Martin (1974), and Ferri and Jones (1979), have all found support for the existence of industry effects on firm leverage. These and other authors argue that industry effects may proxy other variables such as size, asset composition, or risk. Gupta (1969), Toy, Stonehill, Remmers, Wright, and Beckhuisen (1974), Ferri and Jones (1979), and Marsh (1982) examine the relationship between total asset size and leverage and report conflicting results. Gupta (1969), Ferri and Jones (1979), and Marsh (1982) examined asset composition more closely and find that it impacts firm leverage and/or the mix of short and long-term debt. Toy, Stonehill, Remmers, and Beckhuisen (1974), Ferri and Jones (1979), and Marsh (1982) have examined the relationship between risk and leverage and have arrived at conflicting conclusions about the direction and strength of the relationship. Other work, such as Flath and Knoeber (1980), Castanias (1983), Bradley, Jarrell, and Kim (1984), and Kim and Sorensen (1986) have included additional variables as proxies for earnings growth, redundant tax shields, and the size of insider stock holdings. Most recently, Titman and Wessels (1988) extend the set of previously examined factors by including variables which reflect the uniqueness of the firm. These studies provide the foundation for the empirical analysis presented in this paper.

These recent studies provide a wealth of conflicting evidence. This is understandable considering the various methodologies employed and the wide range of proxy variables which are chosen to represent both firm leverage and the independent factors which impact capital structure. There is, however, one characteristic which is common to these studies. They use data which reflect very large, publicly traded firms. In most cases, the Compustat Data Tapes are the source of sample data. By examining the relationships between leverage measures and firm characteristics using data which reflects smaller firms, additional insight into the capital structure question may be gained.

5. Data and Variables

5.1. DATA

The data were collected by the author from the audit and verification files of a commercial bank's asset-based lending department. The initial stage of the raw data collection process involved manually reviewing the entire loan file for each company and photocopying relevant documents. Comparative financial statements provided the financial data. Many of the files had annual financial statements reflecting up to 10 years of operations while other firms only had two or three years of annual data available. In only a few cases were there interim financial statements available. Since recent annual statements were available for all the firms examined, the decision was made to use the end of year financial statements in the analysis.

The financial statements used as a raw data source had identical formats across companies and had been prepared or reviewed by CPA's, thus insuring consistency of account classifications. For 27 of the 35 sample firms, the most recent annual financial statements available were for fiscal years ending in 1987. The financial statements of the remaining 8 firms represented fiscal years ending in early 1988. Due to the small sample size no attempt was made to restrict the sample to firms which reported fiscal year end data in the same calendar year.

Some variables used in the analysis, such as the proxy averages and the coefficient of variation of EBIT, required data from multiple years for their calculation. For 23 of the firms, five years' worth of data were available for the calculation of proxies requiring multiple year data. If the most recent year-end financial data reflected 1987 financial information, the five year period included 1983 to 1987. If, instead, the most recent data reflected 1988 information, the five year period included 1984 to 1988. For the remaining 12 firms, data limitations forced calculations of proxies with fewer than 5 years of data. Of these 12 firms, 4 firms had 4 years of data available, 3 firms had 3 years of data available, and 5 firms had only 2 years of data available.

Due to the small sample size, the decision was made to retain these firms in the sample and perform the required calculation with the available data.

The sample included firms in the manufacturing, wholesale, and retail sector of the economy. None of the firms could be considered to be diversified across different product lines. Descriptive statistics for the sample of firms are presented in Table 1.

5.2. DEPENDENT VARIABLES

Four different measures of firm leverage are examined as dependent variables in this study. The measures are the average total debt ratio (atdr), the total debt ratio (tdr), the long-term debt ratio (ltdr) and the short-term debt ratio (stdr). Each of these leverage ratios are discussed in greater detail below.

The atdr variable is calculated by dividing the average total liabilities by average total assets. Past authors such as Bradley, Jarrell, and Kim (1984), and Titman and Wessels (1988) use average leverage ratios as dependent variables in order to smooth out random fluctuations that occur from year to year. This may be appropriate if the leverage measure is a long-term debt ratio. If, however, the leverage measure is a short-term debt ratio or a total debt ratio this averaging may not be appropriate. If a firm relies heavily on short-term debt financing, both the level of short-term debt and the level of total debt will fluctuate from year to year. Averaging will destroy these annual fluctuations and may obscure existing relationships between leverage measures and firm characteristics. This phenomena may be responsible for the lack of any observed relationships in past studies. In this study, the firms examined rely heavily on short-term debt which is secured by current assets. For this reason, it is expected that an analysis which incorporates the average total leverage ratio as a dependent variable will not prove to be very powerful. Nevertheless, the analysis is included for comparison purposes.

TABLE 1. Characteristic of Sample Firms

Characteristic	Mean	Std.Dev.	Minimum	Maximum
Total Assets	13,121,885	7,878,055	637,000	144,492,992
Total Liabilities	8,060,807	13,640,764	385,500	78,146,928
EBIT	829,105	2,091,462	-950,600	11,603,996
AR Advance Rate	.7957	.0329	.7000	.8500
INV Advance Rate	.3600	.1826	.0000	.8000
Total Debt Ratio	.7449	.1816	.1045	.9749
Long-term Debt Ratio	.1417	.1298	.0000	.3783
Short-term Debt Ratio	.6032	.1662	.0914	.8770
Avg. Total Debt Ratio	.7543	.1262	.3930	.9495

The remaining leverage variables examined in this study are calculated from the most recent balance sheet data and include tdr, ltdr, and stdr. Tdr is calculated as the ratio of total liabilities to total assets; ltdr is calculated as the ratio of long-term liabilities to total assets; and stdr is calculated as the ratio of current liabilities to total assets. Information on these single period leverage ratios and the average leverage ratio for the firms in the sample are included in Table 1.

5.3. INDEPENDENT VARIABLES

Variables representing firm characteristics such as size, asset composition, redundant tax shields, profitability, taxes, and risk are examined in this study. In many cases, both single period and average values for the variables are examined. This is done in order to examine the sensitivity of the choice of specific forms of proxy variables on the statistical results. The calculations used for the proxies are shown in Table 2.

5.4. SIZE

Three empirical proxies representing size are examined: the natural log of total assets (lnTA), the natural log of average total assets (lnATA), and the natural log of average net sales (lnS). Ferri and Jones (1979), who examine both sales and total assets as proxies for size, note that larger firms can carry more long-term debt than smaller firms due to their diversified lines of business activities. Kim and Sorensen (1986), who examine average total assets, note that within the Myers (1977) framework firm diversification is unrelated to capital structure decisions. Marsh (1982), who examines the natural log of total assets, addresses the size issue and argues that larger firms face lower issuance cost for long-term debt and will thus rely more heavily on long-term debt. Titman and Wessels (1988) mention the impact of issuance costs and argue that the costs may impact the composition of liability structure in that smaller firms may rely more heavily on short-term bank debt due to the higher cost of issuing long-term debt. They also cite the Ang, Chua, and McConnel (1982) argument that larger firms have lower relative bankruptcy costs and resulting higher debt capacities.

In this current study, the characteristics of the sample firms rule out any diversification effect. It is also doubtful that issuance costs have a differential affect on the capital structures of the firms due to the fact that the firms' securities are not publicly traded. Size still may be important, however, due to the relationship between size and asset composition. Larger firms in the sample may invest more heavily in long-term assets than smaller firms and may have a resulting need for relatively more long-term debt to finance the investments.

5.5. ASSET COMPOSITION

Four different proxies representing asset structure are used to examine the relationship between leverage and asset composition. Two proxies are used to examine fixed asset structure: the fixed asset structure ratio (FAS) and the average fixed asset structure ratio (AFAS). Two additional proxies, the securable asset structure variable (SCAS) and the average securable asset structure variable (ASCAS) are used to examine the composition of current assets.

The fixed asset variables are similar to those used in Ferri and Jones (1979), and Marsh (1982). It is expected that they will be positively related to the use of long-term debt due to the use of equipment loans and mortgage loans to finance fixed asset investment.

TABLE 2. Variable Calculations

Regression Set I

Proxy   Calculation

LNTA = Natural logarithm of Total Assets
SCAS = (Net Receivables + FinishedGoods + Raw Materials) ÷ Total Assets
FAS = Net Fixed Assets ÷ Total Assets
DPE = Depreciation ÷ Earnings Before Interest and Taxes
ETA = Earnings Before Interest and Taxes ÷ Total Assets

Regression Set II

Proxy   Calculation

LNATA = Natural logarithm of Average Total Assets
ASCAS = (Average Net Receivables + Average Finished Goods + Average Raw Materials) ÷ Average Total Assets
AFAS = Average Net Fixed Assets ÷ Average Total Assets
ADPE = Average Depreciation + Average Earnings Before Interest and Taxes
AETA = Average Earnings Before Interest and Taxes ÷ Total Assets

---

Regression Set III

Proxy   Calculation

TXR = Taxes Paid + Earnings Before Interest and Taxes
COV = Coefficient of Variation of Earnings Before Interest and Taxes
LNS = Natural Logarithm of Sales
DTA = Average Depreciation + Average Total Assets

Titman and Wessels (1988) examine two different proxies: the percentage of total assets represented by intangible assets; and the percentage of total assets represented by the combination of inventory, gross plant, and equipment. Neither of these proxies is appropriate for inclusion in this current study. When the relationship between asset structure and the use of secured debt is considered, a proxy based on intangible assets fails to properly distinguish between assets which may be used as collateral and assets which may not. In many cases, revolving ABL agreements are collateralized by intangible assets and are repaid from the cash flows generated by those assets. The second variable used by Titman and Wessels incorporates inventory and ignores accounts receivable. When inventory is used as collateral in revolving ABL agreements, advance rates are usually much lower than advance rates associated with collateralized receivables. In the current study securable current assets are defined as the accounts receivables and inventory that are eligible for use as collateral in revolving ABL's. Since these accounts are used as the basis for calculating daily drawdown limits against secured revolving credit lines, it is expected that the securable asset ratios will be positively related to the use of short-term debt.

5.6. NON-DEBT TAX SHIELDS

Three proxies are used to examine the relationship between non-debt tax shields and leverage: DPE, ADPE, and DTA. These proxies are included in the analysis in order to provide evidence on the applicability of the DeAngelo and Masulis (1980) argument to small firm debt financing. Existing studies such as Bradley, Jarrell, and Kim (1984), and Kim and Sorensen (1986) use similar depreciation ratios as proxies for non-debt shields while Titman and Wessels (1988) use an investment tax credit based empirical proxy. These past studies report conflicting evidence concerning the relationship.

5.7. PROFITABILITY

Two proxies (ETA and AETA) are used to examine the relationship between profitability and leverage. Titman and Wessels (1988) explain that retained earnings is the most inexpensive form of firm financing. This implies that the more profitable a firm, the less outside sources of debt financing will be used. This relationship should be expected to hold for the firms that are represented in this current study.

5.8. RISK

The current study uses the coefficient of variation of EBIT (COV) as a proxy for firm risk. Previous studies use a variety of different proxies. Ferri and Jones (1979) use the standard deviation and the coefficient of variation of both sales and cash flows. Other authors use EBIT based measures. Bradley, Jarrell, and Kim (1984) use the coefficient of variation of changes in EBIT, Kim and Sorensen (1986) use the coefficient of variation of actual EBIT while Titman and Wessels (1988) use the variance in the changes of EBIT. The usual argument for inclusion of these proxies is that the greater the variability in EBIT, the lesser the degree of acceptable leverage in the capital structure. This study follows recent convention by using an EBIT based risk proxy that controls for differences in the firm's mean earnings.

5.9. TAXES

Kim and Sorensen (1986) argue that due to the importance of taxes in capital structure theory, they should somehow be included in empirical studies of leverage. They include two empirical proxies in their study in order to examine the relationship while noting that any observed relationship between ex-post tax payments and ex-post debt ratios may be difficult to interpret. The current study examines a proxy for taxes. TXR that is identical to one of the proxies employed by Kim and Sorensen for comparison purposes.

The independent variable proxies described above are used in this study's empirical analysis. Descriptive statistics associated with these proxies are presented in Table 3.

TABLE 3. Regression Variable Correlations

			Regression Set I		
Proxy	N	Mean	Std.Dev.	Minimum	Maximum
LNTA	35	15.5490	1.1830	13.4200	18.7890
SCAS	35	.6883	.1912	.1112	.9050
FAS	35	.1844	.1442	.0036	.6711
DPE	35	-.1770	2.0530	-10.0340	1.6460
ETA	35	.0581	.0698	-.0749	.2264

			Regression Set II		
Proxy	N	Mean	Std.Dev.	Minimum	Maximum
LNATA	35	15.3660	1.0350	13.3590	18.4190
ASCAS	35	.4660	.3269	.1104	2.1404
AFAS	35	.1973	.1427	.0065	.6801
ADPE	35	.1630	1.1240	-4.5000	2.3260
AETA	35	.0671	.0449	-.0295	.1481

			Regression Set III		
Proxy	N	Mean	Std.Dev.	Minimum	Maximum
TXR	35	.1243	.2886	-.6013	1.1930
COV	35	.5640	1.0560	-3.7300	3.1870
LNS	35	9.5730	1.0890	7.2700	11.7210
DTA	35	.0388	0.0735	.0000	0.4404

6. Methodology

The methodology employed in this paper is similar to that employed by Bradley, Jarrell, and Kim (1984), and Kim and Sorensen (1986) in that a series of regression models is used to explore the relationships between different leverage measures and various subsets of independent variables. Specifically, there are three sets of four regression equations making a total of twelve regression models. The coefficients for each of the twelve regression models are estimated using the sample data representing the 35 small firms. In each of the three sets of regressions a different set of explanatory variables are examined.

In Regression Set I the five explanatory variables are ATDR, SCAS, FAS, DPE, and ETA. These variables represent the most recent financial statement data. In Regression Set II the five explanatory variables are LNATA, ASCAS, AFAS, ADPE, and AETA. These variables are multi-year averages of the same variables examined in Regression Set I. In Regression Set III the four explanatory variables examined are TXR, COV, LNS, and DTA. TXR and LNS are calculated from the most recent financial statements while the COV and DTA are calculated from multi-year data. While the use of twelve different regression models may at first appear cumbersome, the methodology was chosen in order to avoid potential problems with either multicollinearity or the small sample size.

If all of the fourteen independent variables had been included in a single regression model, high degrees of multicollinearity could be expected between the single year variables in Regression Set I and their multi-year averages that are examined in Regression Set II. This multicollinearity could have distorted the regression results. By using multiple models, strongly correlated proxies can be examined in isolation of one another.[3]

Another reason for the use of twelve different regression models is the small sample size. If a single model with 14 explanatory variables was used with a sample of 35 observations, there would be only 20 degrees of freedom (d.f.) associated with the error terms. By using 12 different regression models with smaller sets of independent variables, each estimated model has at least 29 d.f. associated with the error terms. In each of the first 8 models (Regression Sets I and II) there are 5 variables examined in each model. With n=35 and total d.f.=34, there are 5 d.f. associated with the regression model and 29 d.f. associated with the error terms. In each of the last four regression models (Regression Set III), 4 variables are examined in each regression meaning that with total d.f=34, 4 d.f. are associated with the regression and 30 are associated with the error terms.

As we increase the number of explanatory variables in any particular regression model, the R^2 (unadjusted) increases. In order to reduce the temptation to "pack" the model with additional variables so as to increase the reported R^2, researchers are usually expected to report the "adjusted R^2" in order to take the number of independent variables and the associated impact on the error degrees of freedom into account. In this study the adjusted R^2 values are reported and used as the measure of explanatory power of the various models.

The first set of four regressions examines the relationships between different leverage measures and single year proxies representing size, asset structure, non-debt tax shields, and profitability. The form of the four regression models is as follows:

$$lr = \beta_0 + \beta_1(lnTA) + \beta_2(SCAS) + \beta_3(FAS) + \beta_4(DPE) + \beta_5(ETA) + e \qquad (1)$$

where:

lr	=	one of the four leverage ratios (atdr, tdr, ltdr, stdr),
β_0	=	an intercept term,
β_i	=	estimated coefficients for the independent variables (i=1-5),
lnTA	=	natural log of total assets,
SCAS	=	ratio of securable current assets to TA,
FAS	=	ratio of net fixed asset to TA,
DPE	=	ratio of depreciation to EBIT,
ETA	=	ratio of EBIT to TA, and
e	=	a random error term.

The second set of four regressions examines the relationships between the leverage measures and the historical averages of the same proxies used in the first regression set. The form of the four regression models is as follows:

$$lr = \beta_0 + \beta_1(lnATA) + \beta_2(ASCAS) + \beta_3(AFAS) + \beta_4(ADPE) + \beta_5(AETA) + e \quad (2)$$

where:

lr	= one of the four leverage ratios (atdr, tdr, ltdr, stdr),
β_0	= an intercept term,
β_i	= estimated coefficients for the independent variables (i=1-5),
lnATA	= natural log of average total assets,
ASCAS	= ratio of average securable current assets to average TA,
AFAS	= ratio of average net fixed asset to average TA,
ADPE	= ratio of average depreciation to average EBIT,
ETA	= ratio of average EBIT to average TA, and
e	= a random error term.

The third set of four regressions examines the relationships between the leverage measures and taxes, risk, non-debt tax shields, and sales. The form of the four models is as follows:

$$lr = \beta_0 + \beta_1(TXR) + \beta_2(COV) + \beta_3(lnS) + \beta_4(DTA) + e \quad (3)$$

where:

lr	= one of the four leverage ratios (atdr, tdr, ltdr, stdr),
β_0	= an intercept term,
β_i	= estimated coefficients for the independent variables (i=1-4),
TXR	= the ratio of taxes paid to EBIT,
COV	= the coefficient of variation of EBIT,
lnS	= the natural log of net sales,
DTA	= the ratio of depreciation to TA, and
e	= a random error term.

7. Results

Table 4 presents the estimates of the regression coefficients and the associated t-statistics for each of the twelve regressions included in the empirical analysis. The results are presented in three sections reflecting the three sets of regression models.

When the results for Regression Set I are considered, it is found that the asset structure variables (SCAS and FAS) exhibit a significant, positive relationship to total leverage (tdr) at the .01 significance level (t=4.06 and t=2.97 respectively). This result is consistent with the sample firms' extensive reliance on secured bank financing and lends support to the Scott (1977) model of capital structure. The profitability variable (ETA) examined exhibits a significant, negative relationship to the use of debt at the .05 significance level (t=-1.84). This is as expected in that a relatively more profitable firm will be able to finance its investment in working capital and fixed assets with retained earnings rather than bank financing. The size proxy (lnTA) and the non-debt tax shield proxy (DPE) are not found to be significantly related to the total leverage ratio.

When ltdr is used as the measure of leverage, the asset structure variables and the size variable all exhibit a significant, positive relationship to leverage. The relationship between FAS and ltdr is significant at the .01 level (t=3.74) while the relationship between SCAS and ltdr is

TABLE 4. Estimated Regression Coefficients[a]

Regression Set I

Debt Ratio	Constant	lnTA	SCAS	FAS	DPE	ETA	R²adj
tdr	-0.641	0.044	0.886	0.741	-0.006	-0.801	.310
	(-1.08)	(1.14)	(4.06)**	(2.97)**	(-0.40)	(-1.84)*	
ltdr	-0.797	0.046	0.218	0.048	-0.006	-0.330	.463
	(-2.59)	(2.85)**	(1.93)*	(3.74)**	(-0.74)	(-1.46)	
stdr	0.156	-0.002	0.668	0.257	-0.000	-0.471	.363
	(0.30)	(-0.08)	(3.48)**	(1.17)	(-0.02)	(-1.23)	
atdr	0.492	0.015	0.107	-0.058	0.004	-0.482	.000
	(0.96)	(0.55)	(0.57)	(-0.27)	(0.29)	(-1.28)	

Regression Set II

Debt Ratio	Constant	lnATA	ASCAS	AFAS	ADPE	AETA	R²adj
tdr	0.801	-0.001	0.009	0.139	-0.009	-1.043	.000
	(1.31)	(-0.03)	(0.08)	(0.42)	(-0.26)	(-1.24)	
ltdr	-0.347	0.027	0.024	0.426	-0.003	-0.356	.429
	(-1.33)	(1.53)	(0.48)	(3.01)**	(-0.23)	(-0.99)	
stdr	1.148	-0.028	-0.015	-0.287	-0.005	-0.688	.06
	(2.20)	(-0.80)	(-0.15)	(-1.02)	(-0.19)	(-0.96)	
altdr	0.697	0.009	-0.036	-0.208	-0.014	-0.320	.000
	(1.65)	(0.31)	(-0.45)	(-0.91)	(-0.60)	(-0.55)	

Regression Set III

Debt Ratio	Constant	TXR	COV	lnS	DTA	R²adj
tdr	0.441	0.029	0.010	0.018	0.039	.000
	(0.75)	(0.23)	(0.22)	(0.49)	(0.02)	
ltdr	-0.768	-.0547	0.019	0.054	0.264	.144
	(-2.53)	(-0.82)	(0.79)	(2.95)**	(0.30)	
stdr	1.209	0.083	-0.009	-0.037	-0.226	.000
	(2.29)	(0.73)	(-0.21)	(-1.15)	(-0.15)	
altdr	0.601	0.103	0.032	0.008	-0.456	.000
	(1.52)	(1.21)	(1.01)	(0.32)	(-0.40)	

a = Reported t-statistics are in parentheses.
* = significant at .05
** = significant at .01

significant at only the .05 level (t=1.93). This is to be expected since fixed asset investments are often financed with long-term debt. The relationship between lnTA and ltdr is significant at the .01 level (t=2.85). Since the diversification and security issue costs explanations are not applicable, the size results reinforce the importance of the observed relationship between fixed asset structure and long-term leverage.

When stdr is used as the dependent variable in the regression model, only the SCAS variable is significantly related to leverage (t=3.48). This strong relationship lends additional support to the argument that asset structure is an important determinant of capital structure.

Finally, when atdr is used as the dependent variable in the regression, none of the explanatory variables exhibit a significant relationship to leverage. This is surprising given the relationships observed with the other measures of leverage. The difference is most apparent when the adjusted R^2 values for the four models are examined. The regression using the five single period explanatory variables is capable of explaining 31.0% of the variation in the tdr variable, 46.3% of the variation in the ltdr variable, and 36.3% of the variation in the stdr variable. The same model is incapable of explaining any variation in the average total debt ratio (adjusted R^2=00.0%). It may be that the use of average values in the calculation of the atdr variable smooths the annual fluctuations in the firm's debt structure and obscures the relationships between leverage and the characteristics of the firm.

The second panel in Table IV presents the results of the estimations of Regression Set II. In this regression set all of the explanatory variables are calculated as multi-year averages. Once again, three of the four leverage measures (tdr, ltdr, stdr) are single period measures while the fourth measure (atdr) is an average leverage measure.

In the three regressions which use tdr, stdr, and atdr as independent variables, none of the explanatory variables are found to be significantly related to leverage. In the regression model which uses ltdr as the dependent variable, only the AFAS variable is found to significantly related to leverage (t=3.01). These results lend additional support to the argument that averaging data in an attempt to smooth annual fluctuations in variables obscures existing relationships between firm characteristics and leverage.

The relationship between the AFAS variable and ltdr is the only significant relationship observed in Regression Set II. Since a large portion of the long-term debt used by the sample firms are bank loans secured by plant and equipment, the decrease in the net fixed asset values caused by depreciation charge-offs reflect the payoff of the principal portion of amortized loans. Firms with a lower portion of net fixed assets in their capital structure are expected to have relatively lower levels of long-term debt due to this relationship.

The results for Regression Set III are presented in the bottom panel of Table 4. This regression set examines the relationship between the four measures of leverage and another set of empirical proxies. Two of the proxies (lnS and DTA) reflect variables which were examined in earlier models (size and non-debt tax shields). The two other proxies (TXR and COV) represent variables which are examined for the first time.

When either the tdr, the atdr, or the stdr, measure of leverage is used as the proxy for leverage, none of the explanatory variables are found to be related to the leverage measure. When the ltdr leverage measure is used, only lnS, the proxy for size, is found to be significantly related to leverage (t=2.95). This reinforces the results found in Regression Set I in which another proxy for size, lnTA, was found to be significantly related to the ltdr leverage measure but was not related to the other measures of leverage. Neither the tax payment proxy, the risk proxy nor the non-debt tax shield proxy were found to exhibit significant relationships to the leverage measures.

8. Summary and Conclusions

The results of the empirical analysis provide evidence that asset structure, size, and profitability are all related to the smaller firm's use of debt. Furthermore, the empirical results indicate that these relationships are sensitive to both the choice of leverage measure used in the analysis and the choice of using either single period values or average values for the independent proxy variables.

Asset structure is found to be positively related to firm's use of total debt. Furthermore, the current asset structure is found to be strongly related to the use of current debt while the fixed asset structure is found to be strongly related to the use of long-term debt. These relationships are readily apparent when single period empirical proxies are used. When multi-period versions of the proxy variables are constructed by averaging historical data, most of the relationships are obscured and only the relationship between fixed asset structure and the use of long-term debt remains.

Large firm studies such as Ferri and Jones (1979) and Marsh (1982) have found relationships between fixed asset structure and long term debt. This current study is the first to document a relationship between current asset structure and short term leverage.

Size is found to be positively related to the use of long-term debt when single period proxies are used. This relationship holds regardless of the choice for a size proxy. Since issue costs and size related diversification effects are ruled out by the nature of the sample firms, the impact of size on long-term debt may reflect another factor such as the investment in fixed assets. The relationship between size and long-term leverage is not apparent when multi-year averages are used for proxies.

Profitability is found to be negatively related to the measure of total leverage. This finding suggests that the Myers (1984) view that more profitable firms prefer to fund with internal equity is applicable to small firms as well as large firms.

The proxies used in this study to represent non-debt tax shields, taxes, or variability in operating income are not found to be related to any of the leverage measures. These findings conflict with the results reported in studies of large firms. This may be due to one of two reasons. First, many of the firms in the sample experienced losses during the years used to calculate the proxy variables. These losses and subsequent tax credits may affect the observed relationship between leverage and both the tax based benefits of debt and the impact of non-debt tax shields. Second, many of the lending decisions made by secured lenders are relatively unaffected by short-term variability in earnings. As long as the firm remains a going concern over the long run, the secured assets will provide the cash flow to repay the loan. This is especially true of revolving ABL arrangements where the structure of the agreement forces repayment as the secured current assets are liquidated.

This study has examined the determinants of capital structure for a sample of small firms that rely heavily on ABL financing. The results indicate that many of the theories associated with large firm capital structure theory are not applicable to small firms. The sample is small, however, and may be biased. More work is needed. The methodology employed in this study should be applied to a larger sample of small firms that obtain funds from multiple commercial banks and other non-bank commercial lenders. Furthermore, theories of capital structure that consider the special financing problems faced by small firms must be developed. With more work, a better understanding of small firm operations can be established.

42

Endnotes

1. See books by Clark (1985) and by Robinson (1987) and articles by Stacy (1981), Barbarosh and Tong (1985), English (1986), Gilbert (1986), Herskowitz and Kaplowitz (1986), Pendly (1987a, 1987b, 1987c, 1987d, 1988) and Constand (1987).

2. See Kim (1978), Chen and Kim (1979), DeAngelo and Masulis (1980), Lee, Thakor and Vora (1983), Senbet and Taggert (1984), and Darrough and Stroughton (1986).

3. Examination of the correlation matrices for each of the three regression sets did not reveal any evidence of severe multicollinearity.

References

Ang, James S., Chua, Jess H. and McConnel, John J. (March 1982) 'The Administrative Costs of Corporate Bankruptcy: A Note', Journal of Finance, 219-226.

Barbarosh, Milton H. and Tong, Victor (July 1985) 'High-Ratio Asset-Based Financing in Leveraged Buyouts', CA Magazine, 24-29.

Baxter, N.D. and Cragg, J.G. (August 1970) 'Corporate Choice Among Long-Term Debt Instruments, Review of Economics and Statistics', 225-235.

Bradley, Michael, Jarrell, Gregg A. and Kim, E. Han (July 1984) 'On the Existence of an Optimal Capital Structure', Journal of Finance, 857-878.

Castanias, Richard (December 1983) 'Bankruptcy Risk and Optimal Capital Structure', Journal of Finance, 1617-1635.

Chen, A. and Kim, E. (May 1979) 'Optimal Capital Structure: A Synthesis', Journal of Finance, 371-384.

Clark, Peter S. (1985) Complete Guide to Asset-Based Lending, Prentice-Hall, Inc. Englewood Cliffs, New Jersey .

Constand, Richard L. (November/December 1987) 'Asset-Based Lending: a New Approach to Commercial Finance', Secured Lender, 82-87.

Darrough, M N. and Stroughton, N.M. (June 1986) 'Moral Hazard and Adverse Selection: The Question of Financial Structure', Journal of Finance, 501-513.

DeAngelo, H. and Masulis, R. (March 1980) 'The Option Pricing Model and the Risk Pricing of Stocks', Journal of Financial Economics, 3-29.

English, Robert C. (September 1986) 'Field Examiners: An Untapped Source for Commercial Lenders', The Journal of Commercial Bank Lending, 37-42.

Ferri, M.G. and Jones, W.H. (June 1979) 'Determinants of Financial Structure: A New Methodological Approach', Journal of Finance, 631-644.

Flath, David and Knoeber, Charles R. (March 1980) 'Taxes, Failure Costs, and Optimal Industry Capital Structure: An Empirical Test', Journal of Finance, 99-117.

Gilbert, Frederick S. Jr. (May 1986) as quoted in 'Commercial Finance Takes a New Name and Shifts Focus', ABA Banking Journal, 72-74.

Gupta, M.C. (January 1969) 'The Effect of Size, Growth, and Industry on the Financial Structure of Manufacturing Firms', Journal of Finance, 517-529.

44

Herskowitz, Barry and Kaplowitz, David A. (July 1986) 'Asset-Based Revolvers', Journal of Accountancy, 97-104.

Kim, E. (March 1978) 'A Mean-Variance Theory of Optimal Capital Structure and Corporate Debt Capacity', Journal of Finance, 83-109.

Kim, Wi Saeng and Sorensen, Eric H. (June 1986) 'Evidence on the Impact of the Agency Cost of Debt on Corporate Debt Policy', Journal of Financial and Quantitative Analysis, 131-144.

Lee, Wayne L., Thakor, Anjan V. and Vora, Gautam (December 1983) 'Screening, Market Signalling, and Capital Structure Theory', Journal of Finance, 1507-1518.

Marsh, Paul (March 1982) 'The Choice Between Equity and Debt: An Empirical Study', Journal of Finance, 121-144.

Martin, John D. and Scott, David F. Jr. (Winter 1974) 'A Discriminant Analysis of the Corporate Debt-Equity Decision', Financial Management, 71-79.

Myers, Stewart C. (1977) 'Determinants of Corporate Borrowing', Journal of Financial Economics, 147-175.

_____. (July 1984) 'The Capital Structure Puzzle', The Journal of Finance, 575-592.

Pendley, David H. (January/February 1987) 'Asset-Based Lending Products Within a Deregulated Banking Environment', The Secured Lender, 42-47.

_____. (March/April 1987) 'Asset-Based Lending Products Within a Deregulated Banking Environment - Part 2', The Secured Lender, 30-36.

_____. (May/June 1987) 'Asset-Based Lending Products - Part 3', The Secured Lender, 32-38.

_____. (July/August 1987) 'Asset-Based Lending Products - Part 4', The Secured Lender, 34-41.

_____. (July/August 1988) 'NCFA/Wharton Institute', The Secured Lender, 24-26.

Robinson, David A. (1987) Accounts Receivable and Inventory Lending: How to Establish and Operate an Asset-Based Lending Department, 3rd. edition, Bankers Publishing Company, Boston.

Schwarz, Eli and Aronson, J. Richard (1967) 'Some Surrogate Evidence in Support of the Concept of Optimal Financial Structure', Journal of Finance, 10-18.

Scott Jr., D.F. (Summer 1972) 'Evidence on the Importance of Financial Structure', Financial Management, 45-50.

Scott Jr., D.F. and Martin, J.D. (Winter 1974) 'Industry Influence on Financial Structure', Financial Management, 67-73.

Scott Jr. James H. (March 1977) 'Bankruptcy, Secured Debt, and Optimal Capital Structure', Journal of Finance, 1-19.

_____. (March 1979) 'Bankruptcy, Secured Debt, and Optimal Capital Structure: Reply', Journal of Finance, 253-260.

Senbet, Lemma W. and Taggert, Robert A. (March 1984) 'Capital Structure Equilibrium under Complete Market Imperfections and Incompleteness', Journal of Finance, 93-103.

Stacy, Ronald L. (November 1981) 'Clearance Days in Pricing Asset-Based Loans', The Journal of Commercial Bank Lending, 45-50.

Taub, A. (November 1975) 'The Determinants of the Firm's Capital Structure', Review of Economics and Statistics, 410-416.

Titman, Sheridan and Wessels, Roberto (March 1988) 'The Determinants of Capital Structure Choice', Journal of Finance, 1-19.

Toy, N., Stonehill, A., Remmers, L., Wright, R. and Beckhuisen,T. (November 1974) 'A comparative International Study of Growth, Profitability, and Risk as Determinants of Corporate Debt Ratios in the Manfacturing Sector', Journal of Financial and Quantitative Analysis, 875-876.

AN EMPIRICAL ANALYSIS OF FINANCING THE SMALL FIRM

DAVID A. WALKER
School of Business
Georgetown University
Washington, DC 20057

ABSTRACT. This study provides an empirical analysis of a theoretical model that explains the linkages among the various short-term and long-term sources of financing the small firm. The small firm -with annual sales of less $15 million - depends mainly on short-term trade credit and bank credit and non traditional long-term financing such as owners' personal investments, informal investment, and venture capital. This study shows that bank and trade credit are used as substitutes and how dependent small firms are on non-traditional financing means. The empirical results are based on ordinary least squares regressions on a pooled time-series/cross-section data set of small firms reporting data on the over-the-counter COMPUS-TAT tape. The statistical results leave many opportunities for further analysis as new data are collected, but they show some of the important relationships and methods for analyzing the financing of the small firm.

1. Introduction

The growth and development of small businesses continue to be a primary factor in the longest period of sustained economic growth in U. S. history. Between 1982 and 1987 Gross National Product grew at a real rate of 2.9 percent per annum while the growth in earnings of sole proprietorships averaged 13.2 percent with a minmum of 9.7 percent between 1984 and 1985. In every year since 1982 the growth in employment in small business-dominated industries substantially exceeded the employment growth in large business-dominated industries.[1] The role of small business in the U. S. economy and the effects of regulation on small business have been explored in depth by Brock and Evans (1986). Birch (1987) and Bates and Nucci (1988) have shown the substantial extent to which job creation in the U. S. has been dominated by small business.

If small firms are to continue to develop, it is critical for them to have adequate sources of debt and equity financing and it is essential for public officials to understand how these firms are financed and how to assist them to obtain financial resources. This study presents econometric tests of a theoretical model that the author (Walker, 1989) has developed to explain the financing of the small firm. Most of the previous models on financing the small firm focus on a single aspect of the firm and ignore how these firms use debt and equity in combination. Models such as those developed by Gentry and de la Garza (1985) have analyzed accounts

47

R. Yazdipour (ed.), Advances in Small Business Finance, 47–61.

receivable collections in relation to sales, credit policy and cash flows, and Farragher (1986) discusses the prospects for selling accounts receivables; however, there are virtually no empirical studies that represent the interactions among the various short term debt, long debt, and equity sources that are essential to finance the small firm.

There are two main reasons for the lack of complete empirical work on financing the small firm. First, very few authors have attempted to enumerate more than a few of the theoretical relationships in a form that could be tested. Most of the previous studies have focused on a few financial relationships for the small firm such as profit, revenue, or growth functions. Second, there are very little reliable data available for the econometric analysis. In the few instances where empirical work has been attempted data have been available on only a few variables or only a few small businesses.

Some of the previous literature includes empirical work by the present author on the demand relationships between trade and bank credit (Chant and Walker, 1988), the supply of trade credit (Walker, 1985) and the availability of venture capital for small firms (Maier and Walker, 1987). Gaston and Bell (1988) have projected the size and extent of the informal capital market in the U. S. and estimate this market to be considerably larger than the supply of venture capital to small business.

The U.S. Small Business Administration sponsored a series of studies that inquired into various aspects of financing the small firm at the beginning of this decade. Most of these studies are published in the book edited by Horvitz (1984) who served as the project leader.

Several studies have been completed on aggregate small business financing. Ou (1988) has examined the patterns of financing small business. Other studies completed by the U. S. Small Business Administration and included in their annual report to the President describe the aggregate financing situation for various industries dominated by small firms.

This paper initiates empirical work on applying a model to describe financing the small firm. The basis of this study is the theoretical model that the author has developed previously (see Walker, 1989). The model is summarized in section 2. The methodology for the empirical work and the data are described in Section 3. Section 4 provides the empirical results. Their limitations and the conclusions are presented in Section 5.

2. The Model

2.1. ASSETS

The assets employed by the small firm are virtually the same as those of any firm to generate sales (S) and profits (PF). The firm is assumed to handle its cash and accounts receivable to minimize its outstanding bank and trade credit balances. This allows the small firm to take advantage of trade credit discounts and to reduce bank credit interest costs as cash becomes available.

The primary asset variables which the small firm attempts to manage are:

cash - CA

accounts receivable - AR

inventory - IV

fixed assets - FA

other assets - OA

total assets - TA   (TA = CA + AR + IV + FA + OA)

The asset relationships for the model are delineated in greater detail in the previous study (Walker, 1989). Only a brief description of the relationships is given here. The levels of cash and accounts receivable are determined by the firm's sales (S) and exogeneous factors — credit policy (CP), and the state of the economy, indicated by the real growth of Gross National Product (RG).

$$CA = h_1(AR, CP) \tag{1}$$

$$AR = h_2(S, CP, RG) \tag{2}$$

The change in inventory is the difference between sales and purchases (PR), where purchases are determined by the inventory level and expected sales (S^e).

$$\frac{dIV}{dt} = S - PR \tag{3}$$

$$PR = h_3(IV, S^e) \tag{4}$$

The growth in fixed assets is a function of retained earnings and the exogeneous financing that is available to the firm. For this model these sources include notes payble (NP) - representing long term bank loans — retained earnings (RE), venture capital invested in the firm (VC), and informal investment in the firm (IC).

$$\frac{dFA}{dt} = h_4 (NP, RE, VC, IC) \tag{5}$$

2.2. DEBT

The foci of any model that represents the financing of a firm are the liability and capital components of the firm's balance sheet. Long term debt is virtually unavailable to most small firms, except for mortgage credit that is secured by the firm's real estate and buildings. The primary debt sources of funding for the small firm are:

accounts payable (excluding bank and trade credit) - AP

bank credit - BC

trade credit - TC

mortgage credit due within one year - MC

short term liabilities - STL   (STL = AP + BC + TC + MC)

mortgage debt - MP

notes payable - NP

long term liabilities - LTL   (LTL = MP + NP)

total liabilities - TL   (TL = STL + LTL)

The firm's accounts payable include mainly accruals and is assumed to be constant (AP*), since bank and trade credit are treated separately. Bank and trade credit are assumed to be substitutes that are employed jointly as primary sources of funding the firm's assets. Bank and trade credit are assumed to be determined by the level of sales, the interest rate on bank loans (i), and the cost of trade credit (r). For firms that take trade discounts, r is negative; otherwise r is the penalty or interest cost on overdue trade credit obligations.

$$AP = AP* \tag{6}$$

$$BC = g_1(TC, S, i, r) \tag{7}$$

$$TC = g_2(BC, S, i, r) \tag{8}$$

Little, if any, long term debt is available to the small firm. The short term mortgage credit due within one year is virtually constant (MC*) unless the mortgage is completely paid off during the twelve month period under study. The long term mortgage debt is assumed to be a declining balance of the level of this debt outstanding.

$$MC = MC* \tag{9}$$

To obtain long term bank loans, the small firm will need to show prospects for growth, through

$$\frac{dMP}{dt} = g_3 \, (MP) \tag{10}$$

increasing sales, and it will need to have a satisfactory earnings record.

2.3. EQUITY AND INCOME

$$NP = g_4 \left(\frac{ds}{dt}, PF \right) \tag{11}$$

The major income and equity components for the small firm are:

profits - PF
dividends - DV
taxes - TX
undistributed profits - UP   (UP = PF - DV - TX)
cumulated retained earnings - RE
entrepreneur's capital - EC
venture capital - VC
informal investment - IC
total capital - TK   (TK = EC + RE + VC + IC)

Small firms are price takers in the market place. These firms are not large enough and they do not have sufficient market power to establish prices very different from the market price. Therefore, small firms face nearly fixed prices for the quantities of inputs they purchase and they accept the market price for their outputs. This makes the small firm's profits strictly a function of its sales.

$$PF = f_1(S) \qquad (12)$$

Taxes for the small firm that is a sole proprietorship or partnership are paid as personal income taxes by the owners. For small firms that are incorporated, taxes are a function of net profits, but many of these firms are only marginally profitable.

$$TX = f_2(PF) \qquad (13)$$

With the limited types and amounts of debt that are available to the small firm, the equity of a small business is critical to its sustenance and growth. Initally, much of the equity in a small firm consists of what the entrepreneur is able to invest from personal resources and financial commitments from family members and friends. Small firms pay virtually no dividends (DV) out of their profits (PF); most small firms are proprietorships or partnerships and those which are corporations rarely have excess liquidity and would be ill advised to pay dividends when they are probably facing tight short term and long term credit markets. Most of the undistributed profits or retained earnings generated by small firms for at least their first several years of operations are reinvested in the firm. Thus,

$$DV = 0 \text{ or } DV = f_3(PF) \qquad (14)$$

and

$$UP = PF - TX - DV = f_4(PF) \qquad (15)$$

The econometric analysis of this fifteen equation model is the subject of the remainder of the paper.

3. Data And Methodology

3.1. DATA

The lack of data to analyze the financing of small firms is a well known limitation. Although some researchers have used the Dun and Bradstreet database for analysis of the small firm, these data are incomplete and can only be used for empirical work if very few variables are to be analyzed. After several years of using the Dun and Bradstreet data base for analysis of small firms' activities, the U. S. Small Business Administration has discontinued its subscription to this data base.

The U. S. Small Business Administration and the Federal Reserve are involved in a pilot project to collect balance sheet and income statement data from a large sample of small businesses. Until these data become available, the best sample seems to be the over-the-counter stock firms from a segment of the COMPUSTAT data base. For this study the firms were selected from the over-the-counter COMPUSTAT tape with sales of less than $15 million for which complete data are available for 1982-1985. A firm is defined to have complete data if information is available for all of the measureable variables in equations (1) - (15).

The over-the-counter COMPUSTAT tape includes only 28 firms that have sales below $15 million. There are complete data for this study for only thirteen firms. However, the four years data with a one period lag for some variables provide a total of 39 observations when a cross-section/time-series data set is constructed. Table 1 provides means of some key variables for the firms in the data set. The 13 firms are not very similar although each is surely small.

TABLE 1. Sample Firms' 1982-1985 Mean Values (means in millions of dollars)

Firm Number	Total Assets	Sales	Net Profits	Current Assets	Current Liabilities
1	6.079	1.513	0.131	1.495	0.383
2	6.427	0.015	0.528	0.276	0.985
3	24.322	1.542	1.999	3.228	0.906
4	4.875	7.444	0.141	3.620	1.330
5	1.062	1.865	0.066	0.815	0.394
6	4.216	4.111	0.245	2.896	0.499
7	4.627	7.032	0.250	3.229	1.398
8	1.880	3.906	0.187	1.556	0.568
9	5.496	4.232	1.074	1.382	0.632
10	45.629	11.074	1.797	2.755	6.158
11	22.124	3.485	0.588	1.614	3.038
12	10.122	11.197	0.895	1.424	2.676
13	6.357	4.759	0.190	0.905	0.942

3.2. EXOGENEOUS FACTORS

Estimating the model requires data on several exogeneous variables and proxies or assumptions for others. The real growth rate for Gross National Product and firm's collection policies must be specified. The real growth rates for GNP are: 3.57 percent for 1982-1983; 6.78 percent for 1983-1984; and 3.03 percent for 1984-1985.

To specify the firms' collection policies (CP), each firm's change in the ratio of accounts receivable to sales is examined. If the firm's ratio of accounts receivable to sales (AR/S) was larger for 1982 than the ratio for 1983 the firm is determined to follow an aggressive collections policy for 1983 and CP = +1 for 1983; if the ratio (AR/S) declines between 1982 and 1983 the collections policy for 1983 is defined to be not so aggressive and CP = -1. The values of CP are determined for 1984 and 1985 in the same manner, comparing each firm's accounts receivable to sales ratio for 1983 versus 1984 and 1984 versus 1985, respectively.

A firm's expected sales are assumed to equal actual sales for estimation of the model. If expected sales is a linear function of actual sales, the significance of the parameter estimates in the model is no different whether S_t^e or S_t is employed as a variable in the regression equation.

3.3. ECONOMETRIC METHODOLOGY

The methodology for pooling the time series and cross section that is applied here has been recommended by Dielman (1989, chapter 4) among others. The approach is to apply a transformation to the pooled data of three years and 13 firms so that a set of 39 observations remains for analysis. For the three years (t = 1,2,3) and 13 firms (i = 1,...,13) each observation (X_{it}) is transformed into an element of the pooled data set Y_{it} by the transformation in equation (16).

$$ Y_{it} = X_{it} - X_i^* - X_t^* + X_{it}^{**} \quad i = 1,...,13; \quad t = 1,2,3 \tag{16} $$

$$ x_i^* = \sum_{i=1}^{3} \frac{X_{it}}{13} \qquad i = 1,...,13 $$

where

$$ X_t^* = \sum_{i=1}^{13} \frac{X_{it}}{3} \qquad t = 1,2,3 $$

and

$$ X_{it}^{**} = \sum_{i=1}^{13} \sum_{t=1}^{3} \frac{X_{it}}{39} $$

The resulting data set provides 39 observations to which ordinary least squares regression will be applied to estimate the model presented in the previous section. Note that in equation (16) two means are subtracted and one is added in the transformation of the original data (X_{it}) into the pooled data set (Y_{it}).

4. Empirical Results

The econometric test of the model must be pursued under far less than ideal circumstances. The preferred sample of firms would include mainly firms whose stock is closely held and not traded over-the-counter or in established secondary markets. Small firms whose stock is traded over-the-counter are the best established small firms, and in many ways, they are not typical of the great majority of small businesses in the U. S. For some variables, such as informal capital investment and venture capital, there are no data.

For each of the equations in the model the constant term has been found to be statistically insignificant. All of the t-statistics for the constants are less than 0.50. The largest numerical value of a constant in the model is .0046. For these reasons, the constants in the model are not reported in the estimated equations.

The test statistics that are reported for each equation are the t-statistics, in parentheses under each slope coefficient, the R^2, and F statistic.[2] The reported R-squared values are adjusted for degrees of freedom. It is not surprising that in many instances only a small percentage of the variance of a dependent variable is explained by the hypothesized independent variables. The heterogenity among small firms is one of reasons why there is no established theory of financing the small firm and why the empirical studies of small business are so limited.

4.1. ASSET EQUATIONS

The estimation of the cash equation results in parameters that are insignificant. The conclusion is that either cash cannot be modeled effectively for the small firms or the correct variables were not included in the specification of the model.

$$CA = \begin{array}{c} .2754 \\ (1.11) \end{array} AR + \begin{array}{c} .0357 \\ (0.80) \end{array} CP \tag{1'}$$

$$R^2 = -.01 \qquad F = 0.79$$

Surely a multitude of other specifications of the cash equation could be tested. However, it is more likely that further tests will confirm the conjecture expressed above that small firms maintain a minimum amount of cash and use any excess cash to repay bank lines of credit and loans and to take advantage of potential trade credit discounts that may be available.

The accounts receivable equation shows some of the expected results.

$$AR = \begin{array}{c} .1007 \\ (3.73) \end{array} S - \begin{array}{c} .0559 \\ (-2.13) \end{array} CP + \begin{array}{c} .0049 \\ (0.34) \end{array} RGNP \tag{2'}$$

$$R^2 = .25 \qquad F = 5.23$$

Sales and the firm's credit policy are important determinants of accounts receivable, and these independent variables have the expected signs. More aggressive credit policies (CP = +1) results in lower accounts receivable, and less less aggressive policies (CP = -1) result in larger accounts receivable. Most of the firms' sales result in accounts receivable; the coefficients in the estimated equations cannot be translated into simple changes of a dependent variable for a unit change in an independent variable because of the data transformations that are required to estimate the equations with the pooled cross section - time series technique (see equations (16)).

A reduced form is employed to estimate equations (3) and (4). Information is not available on firms' purchases or output produced nor for expected sales. The estimated equation is the change in inventory as a function of sales and the inventory level.

$$\frac{dIV}{dt} = \underset{(5.34)}{.4657} \; IV + \underset{(1.43)}{.0452} \; S \tag{3'}$$

$$R^2 = .53 \qquad F = 22.48$$

One might expect the change in inventory to be inversely related to the inventory level, but this depends on a number of factors such as recent and expected firm growth. If the inventory variable were lagged on the right hand side, the sign of the coefficient may change; also, the results of the estimated inventory equation might be considerably different if monthly or quarterly data were available for the analysis.

The firms' growth of fixed assets is hypothesized to depend on the long-term financing that is available. Larger amounts of long-term bank financing (measured as notes payable) and retained earnings within the firm are expected to be determinants of the firms' ability to expand plant, equipment, and other fixed assets. The estimated model is:

$$\frac{dFA}{dt} = \underset{(-1.63)}{-1.7869} \; RE + \underset{(10.43)}{1.7802} \; NP \tag{5'}$$

$$R^2 = .74 \qquad F = 55.35$$

A large portion of the variation in fixed asset growth is explained by firms' retained earnings and notes payable. Notes payable has the expected sign, with larger amount of debt supporting increasing plant and equipment. It is unclear why the sign of the retained earnings coefficient should be negative, but the coefficient is statistically significant at only the 11 percent level.

4.2. LIABILITY EQUATIONS

The firms appear to be employing bank credit and trade credit as substitutes as has been hypothesized above. The bank and trade credit equations are:

$$BC = \underset{(-3.40)}{-2.8309} \; TC + \underset{(1.67)}{.1704} \; S + \underset{(.57)}{8.3976} \; i \tag{7'}$$

$$R^2 = .22 \qquad F = 4.61$$

and

$$TC = \underset{(-3.40)}{-.0878} \; BC + \underset{(3.93)}{.0610} \; S - \underset{(-1.00)}{2.5446} \; i \tag{8'}$$

$$R^2 = .45 \qquad F = 11.19$$

Higher levels of short-term credit are associated with higher sales as is expected. The statistical significance of the sales coefficient is much greater in the trade credit than the bank credit equation. This result suggests, as expected, that the relationship between sales and trade credit is stronger than the relationship between sales and bank credit. For some firms sales and the use of bank credit are not closely related.

The interest rate variable in the short-term debt equations is the interest expense on debt as a ratio to the firm's debt. The coefficient of the interest rate is not statistically significant in either the bank credit or trade credit equation. No data are available to construct a measure or proxy for the firms' discount rates on their trade credit.

Short-term and long-term mortgage debt are important sources of financing the small firm. Because of a lack of relevant data, no empirical work has been attempted on the firms' use of mortgage credit or debt.

The firms' use of long-term bank credit is hypothesized to be a function of profits and sales growth.

$$NP = 2.0199 \ PF + .1453 \ \frac{dS}{dt} \qquad (11')$$
$$(0.73) \qquad (1.00)$$

$$R^2 = .01 \quad F = 1.18$$

Obviously, profits and sales growth do not explain much of these firms' use of long-term credit[3]. Part of the disappointing statistical results may be attributable to measurement problems with long-term bank credit, which is computed by subtracting as many capital and other debt measures as possible from total assets.

4.3. EARNINGS EQUATIONS

The firms' profits are a function of sales. As has been discussed above, the small firm has very little impact on the price of its output or the per unit costs it pays for its inputs. The estimated profit function is

$$PF = .1568 \ S \qquad (12')$$
$$(4.82)$$

$$R^2 = .37 \quad F = 23.21$$

In this equation, the coefficient of sales is not the profitability of sales dollars for the firm since the observations are transformed to pool the cross section - time series data.

The tax equation for small businesses is difficult to specify. As in all economic models, taxes are expected to be a function of profits. For the small firm, however, the situation is somewhat confusing. Proprietorships and partnerships distribute their accounting profits to the owners who pay the firms' taxes as part of their personal income taxes. These owners surely must increase the distributions of income to themselves to pay their taxes. Small firms that are corporations pay taxes out of their profits, which often restricts their firms liquidity and what they are able to distribute as dividends.

$$TX = .1778 \ PF \hspace{4cm} (13')$$
$$(2.87)$$

$$R^2 = .16 \quad F = \ 8.27$$

Small firms rarely pay dividends and when they do, often they distribute stock rather than cash dividends. It has been hypothesized that if dividends are different from zero, they are a function of the small firm's profits.

$$DV = \ - .0790 \ PF \hspace{3.5cm} (14')$$
$$(-0.89)$$

$$R^2 = -.01 \quad F = 0.80$$

The regression results in equation (14') support the hypothesis that small firms do not pay dividends as a function of profits and that these firms require all of their available funds for operations. The argument that small firms should hold minimal cash balances and reduce their short-term debt is equally applicable to distributing no dividends and keeping the funds in the firm.

Much of a small firm's profits that are not required to be paid in taxes are kept within the firm as retained earnings. Small firms finance considerably more of their operations and expansion from retained earnings than large firms because small firms have such limited access to traditional debt and equity markets. It is surprising that estimating undistributed profits as a function of profits for the small firm yields such a low percentage of variation explained by profits. Perhaps, including a debt variable as an independent variable in the retained earnings equation would increase the explanatory power of the equation and take account of the small firms' need to use retained earnings as a substitute for the financing that larger firms gain from long term debt.

$$RE = .3170 \ PF \hspace{4cm} (15')$$
$$(2.26)$$

$$R^2 = .10 \quad F = 5.10$$

The regression equations that are presented in this section provide a basis for further empirical inquiry on the financing of the small firm. The limitations of the data and the sample make it difficult to project the prospects of building a significant econometric model for financing the small firm.

5. Limitations and Conclusions

5.1. LIMITATIONS

Obviously the data and the sample size are important limitations of this study. Unfortunately, there are few alternative data sources that are preferrable to the COMPUSTAT data that have been employed in this analysis. Even using data from the smallest firms on the COMPUSTAT tape includes only firms in the sample are traded in the over-the-counter market. Thus, the sample does not include any small firms that are sole proprietorships or partnerships.

There are also some key variables for financing the small firm for which data are not available. Included in this list are: informal investment, venture capital, expected sales, short-term and long-term mortgage credit, and the discount rate or cost for the firms' trade credit.

Using a pooled time-series/cross-section analysis is the only method whereby parameter estimates can be obtained for the available data set. One disadvantage of this methodology is that the estimated parameters cannot be interpreted as simple slope coefficients as one would prefer. If a more complete data set were available, one would prefer to employ a simultaneous estimation technique on a data set that is stratified by size and all forms of organization for small firms.

5.2. CONCLUSIONS

The results of this study are encouraging to those who will continue to explore empirical models for financing the small firm. Some of the theoretical results have been verified in this analysis. For example, bank credit and trade credit have been shown to be used as substitutes in financing the small firm.

Virtually all of the estimated parameters have been found to have the signs that are hypothesized from the theory of financing the small firm. Most of the coefficients are statistically significant, although the percentage of explained variation for the dependent variables is often quite small. The R^2 for models estimated with a pooled cross-section/time-series analysis are expected to be lower than the R^2 valued for a time-series analysis, but the statistical results presented here leave a great deal of room for improvement.

The results presented here should encourage those who have considered investing resources in creating a complete data base of small heterogeneous firms. The data that are being collected by the joint efforts of the U. S. Small Business Administration and the Federal Reserve should provide a unqiue opporunity to develop empirical research on financing the small firm.

Endnotes

1. See Tables 2 and 6, 'The State of Small Business: A Report of the President', Transmitted to the Congress 1988, U. S. Government Printing Office, Washington, D. C.

2. All of the R^2 values that are reported here are adjusted for degrees of freedom and are referred to as R-barred squares in the regression literature.

3. Several similar alternative long-term bank credit equations were estimated. The most impressive result has retained earnings and sales growth as independent variables; only 11 percent of the variation in notes payable is explained by this equation, but the retained earnings coefficient is statistically significant at the one percent level.

60

References

Bates, T. and Nucci, A. (1988) 'High Failure Rates Do Not Typify Small Business Employers', unpublished manuscript. Supported by National Science Fordation grants SES84-01460 and SES87-13643.

Birch, D. (1987) Job Creation in America, The Free Press, New York, N. Y.

Brock, W. A. and Evans, D. S. (1986) The Economics of Small Businesses: Their Role and Regulation in the U. S. Economy, CERA Research Study Series, Holmes and Meier Publishers, New York, N. Y.

Chant, E. M., and Walker, D. A. (July 1988) 'Small Business Demand for Trade Credit', Applied Economics.

Dielman, T. E. (1989) Pooled Cross-Sectional and Time Series Data Analysis, Marcel Dekker, Inc., New York, N.Y.

Emery, G. W. (September 1984), "A Pure Financial Explanation for Trade Credit," Journal of Financial and Quantitative Analysis.

Farragher, E. J., (March-April 1986) 'Factoring Accounts Receivable', Journal of Cash Management.

Gaston, R. J. and Bell, S. E. (1988) 'The Informal Supply of Capital', Applied Economics Group, Oak Ridge, Tennessee. Prepared for the U. S. Small Business Administration.

Gentry, J. A. and de la Garza, J. M. (Winter 1985) 'A Generalized Model for Monitoring Accounts Receivable', Financial Management.

Hill, N. C. and Sartoris, W. L. (1988) Short-Term Financial Management, Macmillan Publishing Company, New York, N. Y.

Horvitz, P. M. (1984) editor, Small Business Finance, JAI Press, Greenwich, Conn.

Maier, II, J. B. and Walker, D. A. (Summer 1987) 'The Role of Venture Capital in Financing Small Business', Journal of Business Venturing.

Ou, C. (April 1988) 'Patterns of Financing Small Business', Presented to the Eastern Finance Association Meetings, Bal Harbour, Florida.

Pettit, A. R. and Singer, R. F. (Autumn 1985) 'Small Business Finance: A Research Agenda', Financial Management.

Phillips, B. D. (October 14-16, 1987) 'Innovative Firms Need Creative Financing', Presented to the International Franchise Associations Meetings, Los Angeles, CA.

U. S. Government Printing Office (1988) Economic Report of the President, Washington, D.C.

U. S. Small Business Administration (1987) The State of Small Business: A Report to the President, Washington, D. C., U. S. Government Printing Office.

U. S. Small Business Administration (1988) The State of Small Business: A Report to the President, Washington, D. C., U. S. Government Printing Office

Walker, D. A. (Winter 1985) 'Trade Credit Supply for Small Business', American Journal of Small Business.

Walker, D. A. (Fall 1989) 'Financing the Small Firm', Small Business Economics.

Wiggins, C. D. and Woodside, B. P. 'Valuing Closely Held Companies: Problems and Issues', Department of Finance, College of Business and Industry, Clemson University, Clemson, S. C.

FINANCIAL CAPITAL STRUCTURE AND SMALL BUSINESS VIABILITY

TIMOTHY BATES
*American Statistical Association
and Department of Economics
University of Vermont
Burlington, VT 05405*

ABSTRACT. This study reports small business discontinuance rates for large nationwide samples of firms that were operating in 1982. Firms still in business in late 1986 were disproportionately the larger scale operations: a strong inverse relationship exists between firm size and likelihood of discontinuance. Econometric models are estimated that seek to differentiate traits of owners whose firms are still operating in late 1986 from those whose businesses had discontinued. Explanatory variables used to differentiate surviving firms from discontinuances include qualitative and quantitative measures of owner human capital, demographic traits, and owner financial capital inputs at the point of business startup. Higher business discontinuance rates are particularly pronounced among firms formed with small amounts of financial capital by owners whose educational backgrounds are weak. The high failure rates that are often assumed to typify younger small businesses were not observed among firms that were well endowed with owner financial capital and human capital inputs.

1. Introduction

This study reports small business discontinuance rates for large nationwide samples of firms that were operating in 1982. Firms still in business in late 1986 were disproportionately the larger scale operations: a strong inverse relationship exists between firm size and likelihood of discontinuance. Econometric models are estimated that seek to differentiate traits of owners whose firms are still operating in late 1986 from those whose businesses had discontinued. Explanatory variables used to differentiate surviving firms from discontinuances include qualitative and quantitative measures of owner human capital, demographic traits, and owner financial capital inputs at the point of business startup. Higher business discontinuance rates are particularly pronounced among firms formed with small amounts of financial capital by owners whose educational backgrounds are weak. The high failure rates that are often assumed to typify younger small businesses were not observed among firms that were well endowed with owner financial capital and human capital inputs.

An article of faith in small business folklore is the notion that most small businesses fail within a few years of their creation. A more recent stereotype of small business has emerged in the 1980s: the nation's small business sector has been recognized as the creator of most of the net new jobs that have come into being in the past decade. These two images—1) job

R. Yazdipour (ed.), Advances in Small Business Finance, 63–77.

creation and 2) high failure rates—have generated concerns about the quality, particularly the stability, of jobs that are produced by the small business sector. If small business has at its base, "a foundation of massive, continual failure,"[1] then the volatility of the small business community may preclude the possibility of sustained employment for much of the growing portion of the labor force that works in this sector. Birch emphasizes this point most succinctly when he states: "Firms rise and fall. Jobs are created and then vanish. Everyone in the labor force must constantly ask: Do I have the right job? How long will it last? What should I do next?"[2]

This study critically examines the premise of massive, continual small business failure. Among small firms with paid employees, discontinuance (or failure) rates are not "massive": they bear little resemblance to the failure rates reported in the recent book by Birch, Job Creation in America. Among small firms with five to 19 employees, for example, annual rates of business discontinuance are under three percent.

2. The Data Base

The samples of business owners analyzed throughout this study are drawn from the 1982 Characteristics of Business Owners (CBO) survey. This data source describes small businesses (and self-employed persons) in a manner unlike any previous large scale survey.[3] The public use samples from the population census data (1980, 1970...) describe self-employed people as individuals; periodic business census data (1982, 1977...) describe businesses. The CBO data base, in contrast, is the first data base of national scope that describes self-employed people as individuals as well as describing traits of businesses these people own, such as sales, earnings, employees, capital inputs, etc.

Among self-employed persons, many are not small business owners according to the commonly understood meaning of the term. Many of these "firms" consisted of individuals—utilizing no paid employees- who were pursuing self-employment on a part-time basis. In an attempt to net out most of these "casual" businesses, I identified small businesses as the subset of the sample where owners 1) had a financial capital investment in the business that was greater than zero, and 2) annual sales of at least $5,000 in 1982. Observations not meeting these criteria were not utilized in this study's econometric analyses. For example, 21,127 responses were received to the 25,000 questionnaires sent to owners of firms classified as "white male owned": 30.4 percent of these observations were dropped because the owners reported 1982 sales of less than $5,000. Of the remaining 14,707 observations, 28.2 percent were dropped because owners reported no financial capital inputs at the point of business entry. This reduced the sample size to 10,556 owners, and 8.5 percent of this group was dropped because of nonresponse problems on certain key questionnaire items. The remaining 9662 owners were connected with 7960 firms, 3513 of which were entered before 1976; the remaining 4447 were entered by owners during the 1976-1982 time period. Thus, 21,127 responses to the CBO survey produced a sample of 7960 businesses owned by white males. This sample is representative—regarding industry mix and geographic location—of all white male small business proprietorships, partnerships, and small business corporations that file tax returns, subject to the constraints that they 1) were operating in 1982, and 2) produced total annual sales of at least $5,000 in that calendar year.

3. Discontinuance Rates, by Size of Business

Table 1 is based upon owner responses to the CBO survey question, "Is the business you owned

TABLE 1. The Distribution of Small Business by Sales and Rate of Discontinuance

1982 total sales revenues	Percent of all small firms In this size category (cumulative percentage)		Percent of firms in this Size category discontinuing Operations by late 1986
under $5,000	38.9%		49.3%
$5,000-$9,999	13.0%	(51.9%)	35.5%
$10,000-$24,999	16.3%	(68.2%)	29.1%
$25,000-$49,999	10.8%	(79.0%)	21.5%
$50,000-$99,999	8.9%	(87.9%)	17.8%
$100,000-$199,999	6.1%	(94.0%)	14.4%
$200,000-$499,999	4.1%	(98.1%)	12.7%
$500,000-$999,999	1.2%	(99.3%)	11.2%
1 million and up	0.7%	(100.0%)	8.2%
all	100.0%		34.0%
all under $50,000	79.0%		39.1%
all $50,000 and up*	21.0%		15.1%

Source: U.S. Bureau of the Census Characteristics of Business Owners Survey; unpublished data. These tabulations are based upon a sample size of 10,148,176 firms (weighted); the sample size (unweighted) is 86,118 firms.

*Small business employers commonly reported 1982 sales of $50,000 or more: rates of discontinuance, by employment level, were:

1-4 employees:	17.6%
5-9 "	13.1%
10-19 "	13.9% (percent of firms in this employee category
20-49 "	9.2% discontinuing operations by late 1986).
50+	3.9%

in 1982 still operating?"; businesses are defined as discontinued if the owner's response was "no." Note that businesses sold to new owners are counted as continuing firms, as long as they were in operation in late 1986: departure of an owner is not equated to business discontinuance in this study. Overall, 34.0 percent of the small businesses that were in existence during 1982 had discontinued operations by late 1986. Among firms reporting 1982 sales of less than $5,000, the discontinuance rate was 49.3 percent, while at the other end of the size spectrum, 8.2 percent of the firms with sales exceeding one million had discontinued operations. Table one clearly indicates that discontinuance rates are inversely related to firm size, with very small businesses accounting for the bulk of the 1982 universe that had discontinued business operations by late 1986.

When number of employees is utilized as the measure of firm size, the same sort of inverse relationship described in table one is dominant: number of employees is inversely related to firm discontinuance rates.[4]

Overall, the smaller firms are consistently the less viable, more failure-prone businesses, while the larger scale businesses are more viable as well as being the predominant job creators. The next section demonstrates that a key element for explaining both firm size and viability is the total financial capital input invested in the business at the point of startup. The balance of this study focuses upon two groups that make up 93 percent of the small business universe; firms owned by white males and females. Minorities are excluded because other studies have shown that the casual relationships between owner traits and firm viability differ somewhat for minority versus nonminority entrepreneurs.[5]

4. Explaining Firm Size Differentials

There are systematic differences across the groups of younger and older businesses, and it is generally quite insightful to divide the samples under consideration into 1) firms formed before 1976, and 2) firms formed between 1976 and 1982. Among the white male firms, for example, disaggregation into groups of younger and older firms produces striking results:

1982 total sales revenues	Percent of firms in this size category discontinuing operations by late 1986:	
	firms formed before 1976	firms formed 1976-1982 period
$ 5,000 - $ 9,999	30.0%	37.3%
$10,000 - $24,999	21.8%	31.6%
$25,000 - $49,999	15.2%	24.3%
$50,000 - $99,999	15.1%	19.0%
.	.	.
.	.	.
.	.	.
$ one million and up	7.7%	19.0%
all	16.8%	26.0%

Similar discontinuance rate differentials typify the younger and older groups of female-owned businesses. The rest of this study focuses upon the younger group of firms: table two's regression estimation exercises exclude firms formed before 1976.

The abundance of very small firms is rooted in the size of the factor endowments available to these businesses. Greater quantities of capital and labor provide the resources that can generate higher sales volumes relative to firms possessing fewer of these factors of production. Factor endowment quality similarly influences sales volume, as does the interrelatedness of larger quantity, higher quality factors of production. For example, the ability of owners to raise debt capital is related to factor quality and quantity. Highly educated and experienced entrepreneurs investing substantial amounts of equity capital into new businesses tend to have maximum access to debt capital sources such as commercial banks.[6]

Factor endowment levels explain much of the size differentials observed among the male and female samples of firms entered since 1976. In particular, females lagged behind male-owned businesses in terms of labor input hours (table three). White male owners possess, on average, more years of managerial experience that women business owners. Females lag behind the white male owners regarding educational attainment; proportions of owners possessing four or more years of college are:

| White male | 35.2% |
| Female | 31.8% |

All of these differences are likely to explain some of the differentials in firm sales (as well as discontinuance rates). In order to identify the relative importance of these diverse factors for explaining business viability, various econometric models are estimated. First, sales are explained utilizing multiple linear regression models of the following nature;

sales = f (owner human capital and financial capital inputs, owner demographic traits, firm age and industry)

Hypothesized relationships between sales and the above factors are straightforward. First, higher quality and greater quantity owner human capital inputs are expected to increase sales. Quality of human capital is measured by two variables: years of formal schooling and managerial experience; labor input quantity for the owner is picked up by average number of hours worked per week in the business. Financial capital inputs are measured by the logarithm of the sum of debt and equity capital invested by the owner at the point of business startup: greater financial capital inputs are expected to increase sales. Applicable demographic traits include owner age: owners at the tails of the age distribution—particularly those over 55—are expected to generate less sales than those in the middle of the age distribution of business owners. It is expected that the youngest firms produce lower sales, other things equal, relative to the older, more established businesses. A related factor concerns business entry via purchasing an ongoing business versus starting one de novo. Purchasing an existing (ongoing) business may permit a new owner to benefit from established managerial procedures; some degree of client goodwill may be present. If this process of piggybacking upon existing expertise is successful, then buying ongoing firms, other things equal, should be associated with higher sales levels.

The dependent variable in the regression exercises is the logarithm of 1982 business sales. The sales variable is a measure of the size and scope of the firms under consideration: sales attempts to measure the value of annual production. Annual sales is really a proxy for annual value added by the firm. Sales is a good proxy for intraindustry data because sales should be a fairly constant proportion of value added within a given industry. Certain industries such as retail and wholesale (trade industries) are typified by value added that is a low proportion of sales, relative to other industry groups. Similarly, construction and manufacturing typically have low value added to sales ratios. This phenomenon is controlled for the table two regression exercises by including dummy variables representing six major industry groups: construction, manufacture, transportation, trade, finance, insurance and real estate, and other services; the excluded industry groups are agriculture, forestry, and "industry not classified".

Firm sales levels and discontinuance rates are both endogenous variables. Independent variables used to explain sales levels in table two's regression analysis are defined below:

Ed2: for owners completing four years of high school, the value of Ed2 = 1; other wise Ed2 = 0.

Ed3: for owners completing at least one but less than four years of college, the value of Ed3 = 1; otherwise Ed3 = 0.

Ed4: for owners completing four years of college, the value of Ed4 = 1; otherwise Ed4 = 0.

Ed5: for owners completing five or more years of college, the value Ed5 = 1; other wise Ed5 = 0.

Management experience: for owners who had worked in a managerial capacity prior to owning the business they owned in 1982, management = the number of years of such experience.

Age2: for owners between the ages of 35 and 44, Age2 = 1; otherwise Age2 = 0.

Age3: for owners between the ages of 45 and 54, Age3 = 1; otherwise Age3 = 0.

Age4: for owners 55 or older, Age4 = 1; otherwise Age4 = 0.

Labor input: average number of hours per week in 1982 spent by the owner working in or managing the business that he/she owned.

Method of acquiring the business - if the owner entered a business that was already in operation, Ongoing = 1; if the owner was the original founder of the business, then Ongoing = 0.

Year in which the business was started or acquired—if the business was started or ownership was acquired during the 1980 or 1981, then Time80 = 1; otherwise Time80 = 0.

Log capital: the logarithm of the sum of debt and equity capital.

Log sales: the logarithm of 1982 calendar year total sales revenues.

Industry groupings: a series of self-explanatory dummy variables is employed to identify firms in six major industry groups: 1) construction, 2) manufacture, 3) transportation (this category also includes communication and public utilities), 4) trade (includes both wholesale and retail industries), 5) fire (includes finance, insurance, and real estate), and 6) service.

In the econometric exercises summarized in the tables below, the education variable group excludes owners having less than 12 years of formal schooling and the age variable group excludes owners under age 35. Firms formed in 1982 are excluded from the regression exercises explaining log sales, because sales totals for these youngest firms cover a different time period—less than 12 months—than the sales figures of the older businesses.

Table 2 reports the regression equation estimates of log sales for the white male and female owner groups. Mean values for all of the table two explanatory variables are summarized in table three. The table two findings indicate broadly that well educated owners investing large amounts of financial capital in their businesses are likely to generate high 1982 sales levels. Larger quantities of owner labor input are consistently associated with higher 1982 sales volumes. Further, the younger firms—those formed in 1980 and 1981—are clearly producing low sales levels relative to the more established businesses that were entered into during the 1976-1979 time period. Entering into an ongoing business—as opposed to starting one from scratch—is associated with greater 1982 sales for all of the groups, but this phenomenon appears to be particularly strong for white males. Possessing management experience prior to small business entry is positively related to sales levels for white males (table two), but not for females. Summarizing the portrait of the male owner whose firm is most likely to produce high sales volumes, he possessed management experience as well as four or more years of education beyond high school level. He purchased an ongoing firm and he invested a substantial amount of financial capital into the venture at the point when he entered into ownership of the business. Finally, he has been an owner for at least two full years prior to 1982, and he worked full-time—at least 40 hours per week—in the small business.

Firms generating low sales volumes are the converse of the above portrait. They are disproportionately female owned and the investment of financial capital into the enterprise is low. Owners of firms reporting low 1982 sales levels are much more likely to work only part-time in these ventures. Finally, many of these firms have been formed very recently, during 1980 or 1981. Several of the most important variables for explaining sales levels performed quite consistently in the regression equations. The financial capital input and the quantity of owner labor input variables showed very high and similar levels of explanatory power for both groups. The time80 and industry variables were similarly consistent although less powerful sales determinants, relative to the financial capital and owner labor input variables. Certain industries were found to be consistently and strongly associated with high sales volumes—particularly the trade and construction industries—which reflects their low value added/sales ratios.

For other explanatory variables such as age, variable coefficients varied across the various owner groups. Owners in the 55 plus age brackets generally produced somewhat lower sales levels, other things equal, but this relationship was statistically significant only in the case of white male owners. Regarding education levels, women owners stand out because none of the highly educated (ed4 and ed5) groups appear to generating sales volumes that are significantly greater than those produced by high school dropouts. The ed4 and ed5 variable coefficients for the male groups are, in every case, either statistically significant or quite close to the significance cutoff levels. The education variable coefficients may be blurred in part by correlations with the industry variables: highly educated owners are consistently heavily over-represented in the finance, insurance, and real estate (FIRE) and service industries.

Tables 2 and 3 in conjunction, explain a substantial part of the lagging sales of female owned firms relative to the male samples. The lower labor inputs and lack of payoff to high education levels are major reasons why the female firm sample produced 1982 sales that were low relative to males. Other reasons for relatively low female firm sales include a higher proportion of firms formed in 1980 and 1981, a lower proportion of owners with four plus years of college, an industry distribution that is service and FIRE oriented, and relatively low variable coefficients, particularly for the management variable. Finally, financial capital inputs are somewhat low in comparison to the white male businesses. Not surprisingly, the sample of women owned businesses was characterized by high discontinuance rates, relative to white males.

As a group, the table 2 regression equations explaining sales levels were well behaved, with all equations reporting levels of explanatory power that were statistically highly significant (F values ranged from 78.61 to 96.79). Explanatory variable coefficients had the hypothesized

TABLE 2. Linear Regression Models: Explaining 1982 Total Sales for Owners Entering Business in the 1976-1981 Time Period

	White male owners		Women owners	
	Regression coefficient	Standard error	Regression coefficient	Standard error
Constant	6.506*	.152	5.914*	.150
Ed2	.063	.066	.032	.069
Ed3	.036	.071	.021	.073
Ed4	.214*	.076	.118	.080
Ed5	.113	.075	.071	.079
Management	.009*	.003	.000	.003
Age2	.004	.047	.025	.048
Age3	-.049	.058	.111*	.055
Age4	-.216*	.071	.053	.065
Labor input	.013*	.001	.011*	.001
Log capital	.340*	.014	.411*	.014
Ongoing	.288*	.046	.171*	.045
Time80	-.258*	.038	-.178*	.040
Construction	.292*	.078	.574*	.115
Manufacture	.439*	.086	.296*	.102
Transportation	.038	.084	.197	.120
Trade	.574*	.069	.458*	.071
Fire	-.039	.091	-.195*	.091
Service	.205*	.066	-.039	.069
n	3657		2903	
	$R^2 = .280$; F=78.61		$R^2 = .377$; F = 96.79	

*statistically significant at the .05 level

TABLE 3. Mean Values of Table Two Explanatory Variables

	White male owners	Women owners
Ed2	.320	.343
Ed3	.211	.242
Ed4	.165	.154
Ed5	.187	.164
Management	5.644	3.677
Age2	.333	.337
Age3	.208	.227
Age4	.123	.144
Labor input	45.895	39.613
Total capital*	$42,775	$40,801
Log capital	9.332	9.074
Ongoing	.244	.261
Time80	.462	.482
Construction	.123	.038
Manufacture	.083	.054
Transportation	.091	.034
Trade	.225	.309
Finance, insurance and real estate	.070	.081
Other service	.294	.391
Dependent variable: Log sales	10.604	10.272
Total sales*	$125,908	$85,724

*these variables were not directly utilized in table two.

signs in nearly all cases, excepting the age variables.

Table 1 clearly demonstrated that low firm sales levels are associated with high rates of business discontinuance. Table 2 factors explaining sales levels are expected to be useful for explaining firm viability in general. Discriminant analysis exercises, reported below, attempt to clarify further the relationships between business viability and owner demographic traits, inputs of financial and human capital, and selected firm traits.

5. Discriminant Analysis: Active versus Discontinued Firms

An econometric estimation problem arises from the fact that entrepreneur factor endowment levels are directly related to firm sales levels (table 2), but they are also linked to each other. In particular, the ability of owners to raise debt capital is related to the values of other explanatory variables. The financial capital structure of the small business at the point of startup is endogenous: stronger startups have greater access to sources of capital; they are less likely to be undercapitalized relative to the weaker startup, which has severely limited access to financial capital sources.

From an analytical standpoint, the interrelatedness of the variables that explain small business sales and longevity limits the interpretation of econometric findings. The objective of this section's discriminant analysis is to weigh and combine the explanatory variables in a fashion that forces two clearcut groups to be as statistically distinct as possible. Table two's regression model, in contrast, sought to establish the statistical significance of the individual explanatory variables. Use of the regression approach (as well as logistic regression or probit models) is suspect because multicollinearity problems may compromise the interpretation of individual variable coefficients. Thus the linear regression model's power to establish variable coefficient statistical significance is sacrificed in this section, but the choice of the discriminant technique produces clearcut results without resorting to violating the underlying assumptions that discriminant analysis is built upon.

This section seeks to clarify further the relationships between owner factor endowments and small business viability; financial capital inputs in particular are studied in greater detail. The discriminant analysis dependent variable measure of firm viability is, by definition, whether or not the business is still operating in late 1986. Businesses that are still operating are active firms; those that have closed down are discontinued, by definition. Explanatory variables utilized in table four and five include the human capital, financial capital, and age variables used previously, as well as several new variables:

1) Leverage: the ratio of debt to equity capital.
2) Time82: businesses started or acquired in 1982 are included in the discriminant analysis exercises.

Greater quantities of both debt and equity capital inputs are expected to improve the viability of small business startups. Scale economies are expected to be operative, thus reinforcing this positive relationship.

Theorists have produced contradictory hypotheses about the impact of debt financing on firm viability. Clearly, borrowers suffer when incremental debt capital inputs fail to generate returns exceeding borrowing costs. Modigliani and Miller have shown that a corporate tax system with interest payment deductibility creates a situation where the value of the firm is an increasing function of its debt—total value ratio.[7] Others have claimed a downside for increased use of debt financing: the present value of the expected costs associated with potential future bank-

TABLE 4. Discriminant Analysis: White Males Entering Business in the 1976-1982 Time Period

	Discriminant Function Coefficients	Group Mean Vectors	
	Standardized coefficients	Active firms	Discontinued firms
Variable			
Ed2	.234	.316	.337
Ed3	.147	.204	.236
Ed4	.395	.176	.148
Ed5	.504	.199	.146
Management	.017	5.703	5.334
Age2	.014	.333	.320
Age3	.094	.212	.181
Age4	-.112	.115	.129
Log Capital	.369	9.411	9.128
Leverage	.028	3.700	3.339
Ongoing	.159	.254	.215
Time80	-.678	.359	.443
Time82	-.720	.155	.229
n		3278	1151

Multivariate test for differences between the two groups:

canonical correlation = .187
approx. standard error = .015
likelihood ratio = .965
F = 12.35 indicating that the group differences are statistically significant;
α = .01 level.

TABLE 5. Discriminant Analysis: Women Entering Business in the 1976-1982 Time Period

| Variable | Discriminant Function Coefficients | Group Mean Vectors | |
	Standardized coefficients	Active firms	Discontinued firms
Ed2	.017	.332	.363
Ed3	.100	.241	.251
Ed4	.122	.155	.150
Ed5	.370	.175	.125
Management	-.021	3.661	3.482
Age2	.040	.345	.322
Age3	-.034	.218	.216
Age4	-.106	.133	.140
Log Capital	.610	9.158	8.789
Leverage	.133	3.261	2.653
Ongoing	-.101	.271	.271
Time80	-.658	.372	.454
Time82	-.610	.172	.229
n		2646	925

Multivariate test for differences between the two groups:

canonical correlation   = .180
 approx. standard error = .016
likelihood ratio   = .967
F = 9.18 indicating that the group differences are
      statistically significant;

α = .01 level.

ruptcy also increase.[8] Not only do expected bankruptcy costs increase with debt, but personal tax considerations which "pass on" the tax advantages prevent many small firms from capturing interest deductibility features of debt. All of this suggests that the basic hypothesis—greater financial capital inputs increase firm viability—may be qualified by a countervailing trend: a high degree of leverage may reduce viability.

The discriminant analysis exercises indicate that the groups of active and discontinued firms are significantly different for white male and female owners regarding their human capital, financial capital, demographic trait, and firm trait group mean vectors. Discriminant function standardized coefficients are reported in tables four and five; the variable coefficients—in standardized form—permit comparison of the relative explanatory power of the independent variables. The exercises are successful in the sense that the active and discontinued firms are shown to be statistically distinct.

In order of explanatory power, the time80, time82 variables are most successful at delineating active from discontinued firms for the white male and female samples; financial capital inputs and education measures are also potent explanatory variables. There are several ways to enter financial capital inputs into the discriminant functions. When equity and debt are entered as separate explanatory variables, both are positively related to viability, with equity generally emerging as the stronger of the two variables. It is advantageous, however, to combine these two variables. Whereas equity and debt each assume zero values with nontrivial frequency, their sum is always greater than zero. Both variables are log normally distributed and their sum, capital, is expressed in log form as an explanatory variable. Use of capital instead of its component parts results in a more precise discriminant function as reflected in the applicable F values. The leverage variable produced standardized coefficients that were distinctly different across samples. The applicable coefficient for white male firms was .028 (table four), suggesting that firm leverage is trivial for delineating active from discontinued businesses. Reliance upon debt capital at the point of business startup is clearly not associated with business weakness or heightened risk of failure. Tables 4 and 5 show that, other things equal, additional financial capital inputs, whether debt or equity, increase business viability, and that the discontinued firms actually utilize debt less than the surviving businesses.

Equity and debt capital inputs are positively correlated (the simple correlation is +.62 for the white male bank borrower group), indicating that these two capital sources are typically complements rather than substitutes. Overall, the more viable firms at the point of startup have greater access to debt: 1) they borrow more heavily than their weaker counterparts; 2) they create larger scale operations; 3) they are more likely to still be active firms in late 1986. Particularly among female owners, the discontinued firms as a group are much less highly leveraged than the active firm group.

While discriminant analysis findings on financial capital and leverage are the most interesting of the empirical results, the very strong findings regarding time80 and time82 are also important. The Jovanovic model indicates that small businesses know least about their managerial abilities at the point where they first enter self-employment. The time82 variable identifies the newest of the businesses in the business samples: among white males, for example, firms formed in 1982—17.4 percent of the sample—accounted for 22.9 percent of the 1986 discontinuances. The same pattern characterized the female groups. The newest firms, other things equal, are most likely to fail and the time82 coefficients indicate that this factor is a consistently strong determinant of business viability. Similarly, firms entered during the 1980-81 period (time80) were more likely to discontinue operations by 1986 than those who entered between 1976 and 1979; they were generally less likely to discontinue relative to those entered in 1982. The longer the period since the owner entered his business, the more likely it is that the business will remain active in 1986. The education explanatory variables produced results that were broadly similar, although differences in magnitude typify the applicable variable coefficients. Owners with five or more years of college were, in every case, associated with active firms, but the education/ firm survival relationship was much stronger for white males, weaker for females. The age variables produced results that were similar for females and white males—owners 55 and older are most likely to be associated with discontinued firms. Purchasing an ongoing business was found to be a shortcut to business viability for white males but not for females. The general insignificance of the management experience variable was an unexpected finding. It may be that a qualitative human capital concept such as this is difficult to measure accurately in simple quantitative terms. Certain traits typify the firms that are most likely to remain in business, irrespective of whether the owner is male or female these include:

1) investment of substantial amounts of financial capital at the point of business startup;
2) possession of five or more years of college education by the owner;
3) being in business for at least three years.

6. Concluding Remarks

Two types of econometric techniques—multiple linear regression analysis and multiple discriminant analysis—have been used to explain two measures of firm viability: total sales (size and scope) and longevity. For the two groups of business owners under consideration—white males and females—certain patterns of statistical findings have been observed consistently:

1. the firm started with the greater financial capital input—other things equal—is the larger scale firm that is more likely to remain in business.
2. for the white male firms (which constitute 72 percent of the 1982 small business universe), high levels of education—four plus years of college—are consistently related to greater firm size and longevity. Among females, this same overall pattern is present but it is not as pronounced.
3. the larger scale firms that are most likely to remain in business are the ones that create most of the jobs forthcoming from the small business sector. Many businesses do fail within a few years of their creation. Among the CBO sample firms created during the 1982 calendar year, for example, 52.7 percent of them had ceased to exist by late 1986. Yet most of these discontinuances were tiny operations that were started with little or no financial capital and no paid employees. No inferences about job stabil ity in the small business sector can be drawn validly from this sort of discontinuance statistic.

Endnotes

1. David Birch, Job Creation in America; New York: Free Press, (1987), p.51.

2. Ibid., p.166.

3. The CBO data base is described in, Bureau of the Census, 1982 Characteristics of Business Owners Washington, D.C.: Government Printing Office, (1987), p.III-V.

4. This point is explored further in Timothy Bates and Alfred Nucci, "An Analysis of Small Business Size and Rate of Discountinuance," Journal of Small Business Management (October 1989), p.1-6.

5. See, for example, Timothy Bates," Small Business Viability in the Urban Ghetto Milieu," Journal of Regional Science (November 1989), p.630-42.

6. This is shown in, Timothy Bates, "Entrepreneur Human Capital Inputs and Small Business Longevity," Review of Economics and Statistics (November 1990).

7. Franco Modigliani and Merton Miller, "Corporate Income Tax and the Cost of Capital: A Correction," American Economic Review (June 1963), p.433-443.

8. M. Brennan and E. Schwartz, "Corporate Income Taxes, Valuation, and the Problem of Optimal Capital Structure," The Journal of Business (January 1978), p.103-113.

9. Boyan Jovanovic, "Selection and Evolution of Industry," Econometrica (May 1982), p.650-653.

ARE THE MOTIVATIONS FOR LEVERAGED BUYOUTS THE SAME FOR LARGE AND SMALL FIRMS?

JOHN C. EASTERWOOD
College of Business Adminstration
University of Houston
Houston, TX 77204

RONALD F. SINGER
College of Business Adminstration
University of Houston
Houston, TX 77204

ABSTRACT. This paper examines alternative motivations for taking firms private. The analysis focuses on the difference in motivations between large and small firms. The study examines the relationship between buyout premiums and proxies for potential benefits form buyouts and the impact of competition. The evidence implies that small firm LBOs are undertaken for different reasons than large firm LBOs. Small firm buyouts are motivated by a desirc to reduce stockholder servicing costs and to diminish owner-manager conflicts. In contrast, large firm buyouts are unrelated to stockholder servicing costs and are loosely related to the proxies for agency costs employed in this paper. There is no evidence of attempted wealth transfer in either size group. Actual or potential competing bids appeared to have limited the ability of buyout groups to systematically underbid.

1. Introduction

One of the more controversial developments in financial markets in the last ten years has been the growth of leveraged buyouts as a means for corporate restructuring.[1] The controversy centers on the unusual role of incumbent managers in many of these deals. Managers simultaneously have a fiduciary responsibility to shareholders to seek the highest offer price from potential suitors and an incentive, as participants in the buyout group, to minimize the bid price conditional on acceptance of the buyout offer. This apparent conflict of interest has fueled charges that many managers have acted improperly and that the transactions themselves are thinly veiled attempts by managers to capitalize on their information advantage and profit at the expense of public shareholders. This view is called the wealth transfer hypothesis. An alternative view holds that LBOs (and corporate restructuring in general) are legitimate mechanisms for improving efficiency and that benefits are shared by public shareholders and buyout participants. This view is called the wealth creation hypothesis.[2]

Section two of this paper reviews the existing literature on the motivations for taking firms

79

R. Yazdipour (ed.), Advances in Small Business Finance, 79–92.
© 1991 *Kluwer Academic Publishers. Printed in the Netherlands.*

private. This section also examines some reasons why the motivations for taking firms private may be different for small firms than large firms. Section three describes and summarizes the data used in this study. Section four presents regression evidence on the relative importance of the hypothesized motivations. The results indicate that wealth creation is an important motivation for both size groups, although the source of gains do not appear to be the same for both groups. In contrast, the wealth transfer hypothesis receives weak confirmation for small firms and no confirmation for large firms.

2. Review Of The Literature

The wealth transfer hypothesis is premised on the idea that financial markets have underpriced the firm's securities and that managers alone are able to determine the extent of mispricing. Managers are construed as using the buyout offer as a means of acquiring the company at less than its true value. Proposals for additional regulation of these transactions [e.g., Brudney and Chirelstein (1978), Brudney (1983), Chazen (1981), and Lowenstein (1985)] presume that public shareholders need protection from managers, principal shareholders, and buyout specialists. The rational response of shareholders to offers believed to be based on inside information and the role of competitive forces in regulating potential abuse is usually ignored.

The wealth creation hypothesis holds that buyouts are motivated by the acquirer's expectation that real economic gains will result from the buyout. These economic gains can arise from three basic factors. First, buyouts usually increase management's proportional ownership in the firm. This increase in the inside component of equity helps align management's incentives with those of outside shareholders and reduces the agency cost associated with the separation of ownership and control. Second, buyouts decrease the number of outside shareholders and increase the proportional stake of each stockholder. This reduces the free-rider problem associated with the monitoring of management and leads to a further reduction in agency costs. Third, taking a firm private may reduce the costs of servicing public shareholders (including the cost of complying with federal disclosure laws, listing and registration fees, mailing expenses, and the cost of public shareholder meetings) as suggested by DeAngelo, DeAngelo and Rice (1984 and 1989).[3]

Most empirical work suggests that wealth creation is an important consideration in buyouts. Travlos and Millon (1987) and Lehn and Poulsen (1987) conduct cross-sectional analyses of samples of firms that went private using pre-offer earnings information and firm and transaction characteristics. These studies find that firms which go private are characterized by poor earnings performance relative to their respective industries and high levels of free cash flow. These studies are inconclusive because of interpretation problems or conflicting evidence.[4] Kaplan (1988b) examines the earnings record for a sample of buyouts and finds that significant earnings growth, relative to industry growth, occurred when the ownership structure was changed.

Easterwood, Singer and Hsieh (1988) adopt a somewhat different approach. They examine the relationship between buyout premiums, pre-buyout ownership structure and the potential for reductions in shareholder servicing costs. That study finds that buyout premiums are negatively related to the fraction of the firms owned by management and positively related to the level of shareholder servicing costs. Both findings are consistent with the wealth creation hypothesis. Easterwood, Singer and Hsieh find no evidence of systematic underbidding in management buyouts (a key element of the wealth transfer hypothesis).

This study seeks to determine if the motivations for buyouts differ between large and small firms. The motivations for buyouts may vary with firm size for three reasons. First, opportunities for managers to exploit an information advantage over public shareholders, the crux of the wealth transfer hypothesis, would seem to be greater for small firms than large firms. Informational differences between stockholders and managers could reasonably be expected to decline with firm size because public information production (analyst following, coverage in the financial press, and coverage in information services like Moody's) is greater for large firms.[5]

Second, the shareholder servicing cost argument as a basis for value creation is more important for small firms. If the costs of maintaining public shareholders contain significant fixed components, then these costs should not be significant for large firms because the fixed costs can be spread over many shareholders. On the other hand, small firms with fewer shareholders do not have the opportunity to exploit the economies of scale in these costs.

Third, the presence of owner-manager agency conflicts may be a function of firm size. One popular argument states that large firms tend to have proportionately smaller managerial stock ownership than small firms. This greater stake of managers in small firms should reduce their incentives to consume excessive perquisites, shirk or make inefficient investments. However, large firms may respond to a greater potential for agency conflicts by investing more resources in mitigating these conflicts.

The agency problem for large firms can be mitigated by providing managers with compensation contracts which align manager and shareholder interests or by erecting extensive internal control systems which limit the ability of managers to increase their utility at the expense of stockholder's wealth. Pettit and Singer (1985) and Fama (1985) argue that, given ownership structure, owner-manager conflicts have more serious consequences for small firms because managers of small firms typically have greater flexibility and discretion in making strategic and operating decisions. This greater flexibility, while not without benefits, allows managers more opportunities to exploit the agency relationship. Thus, whether agency problems are greater for large or small firms is an empirical question.

3. Data And Description Statistics

The data consist of one hundred nine firms which received going private offers between 1978 and 1985. The firms were classified as large or small according to whether the pre-offer market value of equity exceeded $100 million. There are fifty-five small firms and fifty-four large firms. Table 1 presents descriptive statistics for each. The average size of the small firms was $33.7 million. Large firms averaged $543.5 million and had greater variation in value. Table 1 also shows that small firms are largely listed on the AMEX (about 70%), while large firms are almost entirely listed on the NYSE.

The sample can also be classified according to the presence or lack of takeover activity, other than the buyout offer. Included under the heading of "other takeover activity" are outside bids prior to the announcement of the buyout offer, outside bids arising after announcement of the LBO, 13(d) announcements of the acquisition of a large stake (at least five percent) prior to the buyout by an individual or group not participating in the buyout, and a failed takeover bid shortly before the buyout. Table 1 indicates that small and large firms were considerably different with regard to this characteristic. About forty percent of the large firms experienced takeover activity other than the buyout bid, while only fifteen percent of the small firms had other suitors.

This raises the possibility that large firm buyouts are used as a defensive technique to avoid hostile takeovers.[6] This speculation has also been raised by DeAngelo and DeAngelo (1987)

TABLE 1. Summary Statistics

	SMALL FIRMS	LARGE FIRMS
FIRM SIZE		
Average market value of equity ($m)	$33.7	$543.5
Median market value of equity ($m)	20.4	335.3
Range of market values of equity ($m)	$2.2 - $99.8	$109.7 - $4,234
EXCHANGE		
American Stock Exchange	39	1
New York Stock Exchange	16	53
PRESENCE OF OTHER TAKEOVER ACTIVITY		
No other activity	46	32
Other activity	9	22
TIME DISTRIBUTION		
1985	7	16
1984	7	15
1983	13	8
1982	10	5
1981	5	5
1980	9	3
1979	2	1
1978	2	1

TABLE 2. Descriptive Statistics For Buyout Premiums

Distributional Statistic	Small Firms	Large Firms
Mean	51.2%	46.0%
Standard deviation	34.6	24.4
Minimum	7.3	3.4
Lower quartile (25%)	23.5	29.7
Median	40.4	39.8
Upper quartile (75%)	70.7	57.8
Maximum	132.7	130.8

and Shleifer and Vishny (1988). The premiums paid by large firms will reflect, not only the benefits from a possible buyout, but also the perceived benefit to the buyout group of resisting a hostile takeover. Use of buyouts as a defense appears less prevalent for smaller buyouts.

Table 1 also presents a time distribution of the two samples. The number of buyouts proposed in 1978 and 1979 was quite small for both groups but increased dramatically in the 1980's. An interesting difference between large and small firms is the different clusters of LBO offers. Small firm buyout bids peaked in 1982-83 and have declined since that time. In contrast, buyout bids for large firms occurred less frequently in the early 1980's but surged in 1984-85. Note that the pattern of buyouts of large firms parallels the increase in hostile takeover activity.

Offer and other transaction data were gathered from the Wall Street Journal or its Index. Offer premiums were calculated as the offer price minus the pre-offer market price divided by the pre-offer market price. The pre-offer price is the closing price forty days prior to the buyout announcement.[7] Pre-offer market prices were collected from the NYSE or AMEX Daily Stock Price Record. Descriptive statistics for premiums are provide in Table 2 by size group. A comparison of the two columns in Table 2 shows that the distributions of premiums are very similar. The mean premiums for small and large firms are both about fifty percent. The only noticeable differences between the two distributions is the upper quartile cutoff, 70.7% for small firms and 57.8% for large firms.

4. Evidence On The Motivation For Buyout Offers

4.1. MEASURING THE POTENTIAL FOR WEALTH CREATION AND WEALTH TRANSFER

This section examines the relative importance of wealth creation and wealth transfer as motivations for taking firms private. The primary focus is on the different characteristics exhibited by small and large firms. The model measures the potential for wealth creation and wealth transfer among firms in the two samples to determine if the variation in offer premiums across firms can be explained by proxies for these factors and if the importance of these factors differs between size groups. The hypothesis is that premiums paid for buyouts will be directly related to the expected cost savings associated with taking firms private. The statistical association between proxies for potential wealth creation or wealth transfer and observed buyout premiums reveals the extent to which these factors are considered important from the buyers' perspective.

Three competing hypotheses are tested concerning the relationship between the ownership structure of the firm receiving the buyout offer and buyout premiums. First, buyouts may address the incentive problems associated with the separation of ownership and decision-making [Jensen and Meckling (1976)]. According to this incentive hypothesis, managers are more likely to depart from value maximization by shirking, consuming excessive perquisites, or undertaking unprofitable investments the lower their stake in the firm (prior to the offer). Buyouts correct this problem by increasing managers' stakes.

Second, buyouts can reduce the free rider problem arising from a lack of monitoring and control in firms with a diffuse ownership structure. Under the control hypothesis, deviations from value maximization can result when outside ownership is sufficiently diffuse to preclude individual shareholders from monitoring. Buyouts, by their nature, concentrate outside equity in the hands of a small number of individuals and institutions. This concentration of ownership provides incentives for monitoring by these large outside stockholders.

Third, the premium paid for a buyout may reflect the impact of alternative ownership structures on the buyout group's bidding strategy. For example, a different bidding strategy may be required when there are large shareholders that do not participate in the buyout. This is called the bidding hypothesis.

Three separate measures of ownership structure are computed and used as independent variables. The three measures are:

(i)   BOD, the proportion of equity held by managers, officers and members of the Board of Directors;
(ii) HERF, the Herfindahl Index for the holdings of large outside shareholders as a percent of outside equity;[8] and
(iii) AVGH, the proportion of equity owned by the average shareholder (i.e., the reciprocal of the number of shareholders).

These measures of ownership structure are designed to capture different aspects of the conflict arising from the separation of ownership and control. The first, BOD, measures the ownership interest of insiders. It measures the extent to which managers' interest are aligned with that of owners. Thus BOD will be inversely related to the incentive for managers to depart from value maximizing behavior.

HERF measures the concentration of ownership in the hands of a few large stockholders. AVGH measures the dispersion of ownership among shareholders as a group and the potential for the free rider problem to arise. These variables measure the incentives that shareholders have to monitor managerial activity and the degree of control outsiders have on managerial behavior. HERF and AVGH are positively related to outsiders' control and should be negatively related to buyout premiums.

Ownership structure can also affect the bidding strategy associated with a buyout attempt. When outside ownership is atomistic (small HERF and AVGH), Shleifer and Vishny's (1986) analysis of takeover bidding implies that buyout premiums will be inversely related to the

TABLE 3. The Hypothesized Relationships Between Premiums And Measures Of Ownership Structure

Hypothesis	BOD	AVGH	HERF
Incentive	-	0	0
Control	0	-	-
Bidding	-	0	+

proportion of inside ownership. On the other hand, when outside ownership is not atomistic (large HERF), bidding strategies involve a bargaining game between insiders and outsiders. Fishman (1988) shows that an initial bidder may make a preemptive offer when there is a serious threat of a competing bid. Concentrated outside holders can bargain with the buyout group and could launch or solicit counter offers. The possibility of these actions would encourage a higher offer price in Fishman's model. These bidding arguments imply that premiums should be negatively related to BOD and positively related to HERF. Table 3 summarizes alternative hypotheses regarding the relationship between premiums and the firm's ownership structure.

The other source of potential wealth creation is a reduction in shareholder servicing costs [see DeAngelo, DeAngelo and Rice (1984 and 1989)]. The variable relative listing cost, RLC, is designed to proxy for the level of shareholder servicing costs. RLC is calculated by scaling the annual listing expense, per the NYSE and AMEX fee schedules, by each firm's (preoffer) market value of equity. Both fee schedules are increasing and stepwise concave functions of the number of shares outstanding. Scaling by firm size produces a measure of the average servicing cost per dollar of equity which declines with firm size (i.e., displays economies of scale in servicing shareholders). Since the listing fee is but a small portion of shareholder servicing expenses and is itself a small absolute amount, significant results should be obtained only if RLC varies proportionately with the sum of all such costs.

Finally, the wealth transfer hypothesis predicts that managers can exploit inside information by engaging in buyouts when outsiders undervalue the firm (or the proposed improvement in the firm). This argument assumes that outsiders cannot infer the existence of underpricing from the buyout offer, and/or cannot launch competing bids for the firm. If this analysis is correct, then we should find systematically lower offers, ceteris paribus, in the absence of competing bids. In order to examine this hypothesis we include a dummy variable, TKB, that takes the value one if there are other bids competing with the buyout offer, and zero otherwise. The wealth transfer hypothesis predicts a positive coefficient for TKB.

4.2. EVIDENCE

The importance of the above hypotheses are examined by regressing buyout offer premiums against the proxies for wealth creation, wealth transfers, and alternative bidding strategies. Table 4 presents regression coefficients run on two separate subsamples classified by firm size.[9]

For the small firm sample, the coefficients on the proxies for stockholder servicing costs

TABLE 4. Regressions Of Buyout Premiums On Proxies Of The Potential For Wealth Creation
And Wealth Transfer

Variable	Small Firms		Large Firms	
	Equation (1)	Equation (2)	Equation (1)	Equation (2)
Intercept	0.422	0.344	0.420	0.462
	(4.48)	(4.18)	(4.02)	(5.19)
RLC	219.43	202.69	300.81	359.89
	(5.56)	(4.98)	(1.05)	(1.30)
BOD	-0.432	——	-0.111	——
	(-2.24)		(-0.38)	
AVGH	——	-107.40	——	-408.83
		(-1.54)		(-1.97)
HERF	0.142	0.594	-0.722	1.788
	(0.35)	(1.45)	(-0.54)	(1.01)
TKB	-0.035	0.026	-0.032	-0.071
	(-0.34)	(0.26)	(-0.39)	(-0.08)
F-statistic	9.069	8.039	0.378	1.343
	(0.001)	(0.001)	(0.823)	(0.268)
Adjusted R^2	0.374	0.343	-0.050	0.026

T-statistics are under the coefficient estimates, and a significance level is under the F-statistic.

Variables in regression equations (1) and (2)

RLC = Relative Listing Cost
BOD = Proportional holdings by officers, members of the Board of Directors and other top
managers
AVGH = Average stockholdings (proportion); reciprocal of number of stockholders
HERF = Herfindahl Index for holdings of large, non-managerial shareholders; the
Herfindahl Index is the sum of the squared percentage holdings.
BT = Buyout type
= 0 if buyout group does not include incumbent managers
= 1 if buyout group includes incumbent managers

(RLC) and managerial incentive problems (BOD) are significant and of the predicted sign. That is, buyout premiums, for small firms, are increasing in relative listing costs and decreasing in management's pre-offer stake in the firm. The coefficients on the concentration of outside ownership (HERF) and the potential for the free-rider problem (AVGH) have the predicted sign but are statistically insignificant. These results do not provide confirmation of the role of the concentration of outside ownership in monitoring managers or in the bidding process in the market for corporate control.

The results from the large firm group are substantially different. The coefficients on the stock-holder servicing cost variable, the proxy for managerial incentive problems, the concentration of outside ownership, and the takeover dummy are all insignificant. Only the variable measuring the overall dispersion of ownership, AVGH, is significant. The coefficient on AVGH is negative implying that buyouts of large firms may be induced by a desire to improve monitoring and control of management.

The coefficient on the presence of other takeover activity, TKB, is insignificant in both regressions. This finding provides no support for the views that there is a lack of competition in LBOs or that explicit competition is required to elicit higher prices. Apparently, the presence or threat of competing bids for both size groups was sufficient to prevent systematic underbidding by managers. Potential competition will figure heavily in the bidding strategy of any buyout group.[10] Thus buyout groups either (irrationally) ignore the lack of competition or are offering competitive premiums. Therefore, this result implies rejection of the wealth transfer hypothesis.[11]

A comparison of the results reveals that there are three major differences between small and large firms: (i) the importance of listing costs, (ii) the importance of the measure of managers' incentives to act in the stockholders' interest, (iii) the overall ability of the regression model to explain buyout premiums. Relative listing costs has a strong, positive relationship with buyout premiums for small firms and an insignificant relationship with premiums for large firms.[12] This pronounced difference is not surprising because the dollar value of shareholder servicing costs hardly seems capable of explaining the multi-million dollar premiums offered for larger firms. However, this type of cost savings is plausible as a motivation for converting to private ownership for companies with only a few million dollars of equity.

The insignificant relationship between BOD, a proxy for managerial incentives in the large firm, is in contrast with the significant negative relationship in the small firm sample. This finding could be viewed as evidence that the conflict of interest between stockholders and management is less important for large firms than to the small. These results, however, must be interpreted with caution. The variable, BOD, may simply be more appropriate as a proxy for the incentives of managers to maximize firm value for small firms than large. BOD may be a misleading measure of managers' incentives for large firms for three reasons. First, the use of stock options and other aspects of optimal incentive contracts may be more pervasive among large firms. The managers that have such compensation packages may be induced to act in the interest of shareholders regardless of their proportional holdings. Second, internal control procedures in large organizations could provide effective monitoring against value reducing behavior by managers. That is, large firms may choose to mitigate agency conflicts through monitoring instead of bonding. Failure to account for differences in internal control mechanisms between large firms might make BOD an inappropriate indicator.[13] Third, the capital needs of large firms and the wealth constraints faced by managers could make such fractional measures of ownership misleading.

The explanatory power of the models differs substantially between the two size groups. The regression models perform well for small firms, explaining about thirty-five percent of the variation in buyout premiums. In contrast, the models explain almost none of the variation in premiums for large firms. One plausible explanation of this difference between size groups is that the use of buyouts as a defensive mechanism against hostile takeovers injects substantial variation in premiums for large firms. Premiums in such cases will reflect the value managers attach to controlling their own environment in addition to the savings from converting the firm to private ownership. This complication appears to be a potential problem for the sample of large firms, but not for the sample of small firms.

5. Summary

This paper examines alternative motivations for taking firms private. The analysis focuses on the difference in motivations between large and small firms. Firms are categorized as small if the pre-offer market value of equity is less than $100 million and large otherwise. Using a sample of 109 buyout offers made between 1978 and 1985, the study examines the relationship between buyout premiums and proxies for potential benefits from buyouts and the impact of competition.

The evidence implies that small firm LBOs are undertaken for different reasons than large firm LBOs. In particular, small firm buyouts are motivated by a desire to reduce stockholder servicing costs and diminish owner-manager conflicts. On the other hand, reduction of stockholder servicing costs does not appear to be an important motivation for large firm buyouts. There is, however, some evidence consistent with an agency cost argument for large firms. There is no evidence of attempted wealth transfer in either size group. Actual or potential competing bids appeared to have limited the ability of buyout groups to systematically underbid.

Endnotes

1. Throughout this paper we use the term going private and leveraged buyouts synonymously. Unfortunately, the use of these terms varies some between authors. All of the transactions included in this paper involved the purchase of all outstanding stock (or stock not owned by members of the buyout group) by a manager, group of managers, or principal shareholders. Most of these deals were financed with a high degree of leverage.

2. A third view, not examined in this paper, is that firms are, at least in part, motivated to convert to private ownership because of the possibility of stepping up the basis of existing assets and realizing substantial tax benefits. See Lowenstein (1985 and 1986),Lehn and Poulsen (1987), DeAngelo and DeAngelo (1987), Shleifer and Vishny (1988), and Kaplan (1988a) for a discussion of this issue.

3. The difference between the wealth transfer hypothesis and the wealth creation hypothesis is that the latter is motivated by the creation of real economic value through restructuring, whereas the former is motivated by inside information about either the current value of the firm or the value of the proposed changes in the firm. Therefore, buyouts motivated by wealth transfers will not occasion premiums that reflect the value of the inside information. On the other hand, the premiums paid in buyouts motivated by wealth creation will reflect the real economic gains associated with the buyout. Of course, some buyouts (perhaps most) are motivated by a combination of these two motives. The intent of this paper is to determine the relative strength of these motivations among small versus large firms.

4. For example, Lehn and Poulsen find that the relationship between free cash flow and buyout premiums is strong (weak) for firms with concentrated (diffuse) ownership structures. This unusual finding would appear to contradict an agency explanation.

5. For example, Kross (1985) finds that the correlation between firm size and Wall Street Journal Coverage is 0.99. The greater information production for large firms than small has also been shown to affect the ability of markets to forecast firm specific information and the speed of adjustment to information release. See Grant (1980), Freeman (1987), and Chari, Jaganathan and Ofer (1988) for evidence on the impact of firms size in the case of earnings announcements.

6. Jensen (1986) contends that takeovers are motivated by the same factors motivating buyouts. If correct, the buyout premiums will also reflect these factors, even if the overriding motivation of the buyout group is to defend against a hostile takeover. However, it is unlikely that reduction of shareholder servicing costs could be an important motivation for a hostile takeover attempt.

7. In those cases where other takeover activity occurred, the relevant announcement date was the first announcement of any type of takeover activity. If the buyout group revised its bid in response to shareholder litigation or to negotiations with management (outside directors if management participates in the offer), the final offer price was chosen.

8. The Herfindahl Index is the sum of the squared proportionate holdings of large outside-

shareholders (with at least a five percent stake). The maximum number of these shareholders in the two samples were five.

9. The evidence presented in this paper is suggestive in nature. The comparison of regressions does not constitute a statistical test of the hypothesis that motivations differ across size groups. The conventional approaches to such a test are either (i) separate regressions with t-tests for differences in coefficients between the regressions, or (ii) a single regression with additive and multiplicative dummy variables for the size groupings. Both approaches require that the distributions of the independent variables be the same for the two size groups. This requirement is violated. For example, the empirical distributions of listing costs are quite different between groups. See endnotes 12.

10. The less frequent arrival of a competing bidder for the sample of small firms, as shown in Table 1, does not necessarily provide evidence of a lack of competition.

11. The evidence that premiums are decreasing in management pre-offer ownership of the firm could also imply that managers can underbid when they have a high degree of voting control. However, control must be judged in relation to actual or potential outside competition. Thus these results along with the result that premiums are not related to the degree of competition support the wealth creation explanation rather than the wealth transfer hypothesis.

12. The absolute size of the coefficients for the two size groups reflects the relative size of this variable for each group. The average ratio of listing costs to pre-offer market value of equity for small firms is over four times as large as the average ratio for large firms. The standard deviation of relative listing costs for small firms is more than eight times the standard deviation for large firms.

13. See Pettit and Singer (1985) and Fama (1985).

References

Amihud, Yakov (1988) 'Management Buyouts and Shareholders' Wealth', presented at the Conference on Management Buyouts, sponsored by the Salomon Brothers Center for the Study of Financial Institutions.

Brudney, Victor (July 1983) 'Equal Treatment of Shareholders in Corporate Distributions and Reorganizations', California Law Review, 1072-1092.

Brudney, Victor and Chirelste, Marvin (June 1978) 'A Restatement of Corporate Freezeouts', Yale Law Journal, 1354-1376.

Chari, V., Jaganathan, Ravi and Ofer, Robert (May 1988) 'Seasonalities in Security Returns: The Case of Earnings Announcements', Journal of Financial Economics, 101-122.

Chazen, Leonard (July 1981) 'Fairness from a Financial Point of View in Acquisitions of Public Companies: 'Is 'Third-Party Sale Value' the Appropriate Standard?', Business Lawyer, pp.1439-1481.

DeAngelo, Harry, DeAngelo, Linda and Rice, Edward (October 1984) 'Going Private: Minority Freezeouts and Stocholder Wealth', Journal of Law and Economics, 367-401.

DeAngelo, Harry, DeAngelo, Linda and Rice, Edward (1989) 'Going Private: The Effects of a Change in Corporate Ownership Structure', in Corporate Restructuring and Executive Compensation, Joel M. Stern, G. Bennett Stewart III and Donald H. Chew,Jr., ed., Ballinger Publishing Company.

Easterwood, John, Singer, Ronald and Hsieh, Vivian (1988) 'The Motivations for Going Private', mimeo, University of Houston.

Fishman, Michael (Spring 1988) 'A Theory of Preemptive Takeover Bidding', Rand Journal of Economics, 88-101.

Fama, Eugene (January 1985) 'What's Different about Banks?', Journal of Monetary Economics.

Freeman, R.N. (1987) 'The Association between Accounting Earnings and Security Returns for Large and Small Firms', Journal of Accounting and Economics 9, 195-225.

Grant, Edward (1980) 'Market Implications of Differential Amounts of Interim Information', Journal of Accounting Research 18, 255-268.

Jensen, Michael (May 1986) 'Agency Costs of Free Cash Flow, Corporate Finance, and Takeovers', American Economic Review, 326-329.

Jensen, Michael and Meckling, William (October 1976) 'Theory of the Firm: Managerial Behavior, Agency Costs, and Ownership Structure', Journal of Financial Economics, 305-360.

Kaplan, Steven (September 1988a) 'Management Buyouts: Evidence on Taxes as a Source of Value', Working Paper #245, Center for Research on Security Prices.

Kaplan, Steven (October 1988b) 'Management Buyouts: Efficiency Gains or Value Transfers', Working Paper #244, Center for Research on Security Prices.

Kross, W. (1985) 'Firm Prominence and Differential Information Content of Quarterly Earnings Announcements', Working Paper, Purdue University.

Lehn, Kenneth and Annette Poulsen (February 1987) 'Sources of Value in Leveraged Buyouts', mimeo, Securities and Exchange Commission.

Lowenstein, Louis (May 1985) 'Management Buyouts', Columbia Law Review, 730-784.

Lowenstein, Louis (January/February 1986) 'No More Cozy Management Buyouts', Harvard Business Review, 147-156.

Pettit, Richardson and Singer, Ronald (Autumn 1985) 'Small Business Finance: A Research Agenda', Financial Management, 47-60.

Shleifer, Andrei and Vishny, Robert (June 1986) 'Large Shareholders and Corporate Control', Journal of Political Economy, 461-488.

Shleifer, Andrei and Vishny, Robert (1988) 'Management Buyouts as a Response to Market Pressure', in Mergers and Acquisitions, Alan Auerbach (ed.), National Bureau of Economic Research, University of Chicago, pp.87-102.

Travlos, Nickolaos and Millon, Marcia (April 1987) 'Going Private Buyouts and Determinants of Shareholder Returns', Working Paper 87-6, Center for the Study of Financial Institutions and Markets, Southern Methodist University.

FINANCIAL ISSUES IN FRANCHISING

EDWARD A. DYL
Karl Eller Graduate School of Management
University of Arizona
Tucson, Arizona 85721

ABSTRACT. This study examines franchising as a form of business organization. A model is developed illustrating how franchising both reduces agency costs that would be associated with the use of company-employed managers and permits franchisors to expand more rapidly than would be possible using company-owned units. The former factor appears to be the primary explanation for the success of franchising as an organizational form.

1. Introduction

Franchising is an interesting form of economic organization in that it is widespread but not well-understood. Franchisees account for a large proportion of the total goods and services produced in the United States and they represent a large proportion of the total number of small businesses in the United States (see Kostecka (1985)). Similarly, franchising is an important vehicle for the creation of "new" small businesses in the sense that it enables potential entrepreneurs to become owner-managers of their own businesses. However, to date there has been no clear explanation of why so much of the entrepreneurial activity in our economy takes place under franchising arrangements. This paper analyses the advantages of franchising as an organizational form, and offers some explanations for franchising that have not been considered heretofore.

It appears that some products or services are more "franchisable" than others. Products or services that are well-suited to franchising generally have three basic characteristics: (1) the trademark on the product or service is of considerable value in and of itself, presumably because the trademark signals something to the consumer about the nature of and/or quality of the product or service; (2) production and/or distribution of the product or service can be decentralized among many small units without resulting in any important or significant diseconomies of scale; and (3) the product or service is best supplied to consumers at or near the site of consumption. (Caves and Murphy Page 2 (1976) provide a further discussion of the characteristics of franchising.) However, the simple fact that some products and services are more suited to franchising arrangements than others is not sufficient to explain the existence of franchising as an organizational form. That is, although a potential franchisor always has the opportunity to lease his/her trademark to a franchisee, presumably the franchisor will only do this when the franchise form of organization has an advantage over the alternative of the firm producing and distributing the product or service through an equal number of decentralized wholly-owned

R. Yazdipour (ed.), Advances in Small Business Finance, 93–107.

subsidiaries.

Most early studies of franchising organizations concluded that the primary motivation for franchising was that it served as a means for the franchisor to raise additional capital for expansion, since most of the investment capital for a franchised unit is provided by the franchisee. (see Oxenfeldt and Thompson (1968-69), Hunt (1973), and Caves and Murphy (1976)). However, Rubin (1978) does an excellent job of demolishing this notion as follows:

> A consideration of this argument in the light of modern capital market theory quickly indicates that it is fallacious. A franchisor will own outlets in many areas; a franchisee will in general own only one or a few outlets in the same area. Thus, the investment of the franchisee will be much riskier than the overall franchise chain. A risk averse franchisee would clearly prefer to invest in a portfolio of shares in all franchise outlets, rather than confirming his investment to a single store. (p. 225)

The "capital for expansion" explanation for the existence of franchising is clearly inconsistent with our current understanding of risk aversion and portfolio diversification.

Rubin (1978) then proceeds to explain the existence of franchising in terms of the well-known agency problem.[2] Because agents (e.g., employees) frequently have incentives to engage in actions that are not in the best interests of the principal (e.g., the firm), firms will incur costs to control and monitor the agents' behavior. These costs may be especially large for firms that engage in the types of businesses that we have characterized as "franchisable," where the production and distribution of the product or service is geographically decentralized and therefore not easily controlled by the firm's central management. At a minimum, the costs of controlling and monitoring operations will be unusually high in these firms relative to a "typical" firm. Rubin suggests that franchising may represent a least-cost solution to the agency problem for certain types of firms. In a recent and insightful paper, Brickley and Dark (1987) present some empirical evidence that the agency costs resulting from geographical decentralization are relevant to the franchisor's choice between a franchisee-owned versus a company-owned unit at a given location, a finding which supports Rubin's analysis.

The analysis of franchising presented in this paper is based heavily, although not entirely, on the agency considerations discussed by Rubin (1978) and Brickley and Dark (1987). In particular, we suggest that there are two agency-related factors that make the franchise form of organization advantageous in certain situations. First, franchising may permit the "parent" firm (i.e., the franchisor) to expand at a more rapid rate than would be possible through wholly-owned subsidiaries, although for reasons that have nothing to do with the availability of capital, and, second, the franchise agreement may be an inherently efficient solution to the basic agency problem simply due to the nature of small, owner-operated businesses.

2. The Growth of the Firm

The primary limitation on the rate at which a firm can expand is related to the complex nature of organizations. Managerial considerations stemming from organizational complexity pose barriers to the rapidity with which a firm can expand, even in the presence of perfect capital and labor markets. Adding new members (e.g., managers and lower-level employees) to an organization involves more than simply hiring and training them—although the hiring process poses a barrier to expansion in and of itself, especially with regard to expansion at the managerial level. New employees must also be integrated into the social fabric of the organization and inculcated with the organization's values and behavioral and ethical expectations. They must be supervised by earlier members of the organization who have advanced to the level of managers, and the rate at which the organization can expand its cadre of such managers may be limited. This whole process is the primary limitation on the rate at which an organization can expand. Copeland and Weston (1985, p. 55), in their discussion of capital rationing, refer to this problem as the "Penrose effect" after Edith Penrose's classic book on the subject of the growth of the firm (see Penrose (1959)). Franchising may provide a means of avoiding, or at least relaxing, these constraints on the firm's rate of growth by permitting the firm to add productive capacity without requiring the same degree of overall organizational expansion (especially at the managerial level) that would be needed for internal growth.

2.1. A MODEL OF THE GROWTH CONSTRAINT

In this section we develop a simple theoretical model of the effect of the growth constraint on the value of the firm. Consider a firm that produces a franchisable product or service (hereafter referred to simply as the product). Assume a world of certainty where the firm initially produces and distributes the product through company-owned units that are homogeneous with regard to sales and costs and further assume that once an operating unit is established it generates cash flows in perpetuity. The net present value of each of these company-owned operating units may be denoted as follows:

$$P_c = \frac{[\, S_c\,(\,1 - C_c\,) - m_c\,]}{k_c} - I \tag{1}$$

where:

P_c = the net present value of the company-owned unit,
S_c = the sales of the unit per period,
C_c = the variable cost of production expressed as a percentage of sales,
m_c = the dollar cost of controlling and monitoring the managers at each decentralized company-owned unit,
k_c = the appropriate discount rate for this stream of cash flows, and
I = the initial investment required to establish each unit.

For simplicity, we assume that there are no fixed costs of production beyond the initial investment, I.

The net present value of the firm at a given time (V_t) will be equal to the number of units in operation (N_t) times the value per unit (P_c) plus the discounted value of additional units to be established in the future. This latter component of the firm's total value may be thought of as the present value of the firm's growth opportunities, which would be known to investors in the certain world assumed for our model. The existence of such growth opportunities is an important component of the total value of a firm (see, for example, Brealey and Myers (1988, pp. 57-60)).

The initial value of the firm can therefore be expressed as:

$$V_0 = N_0 (P_c) + \sum_{t=1}^{T} \frac{n_t (P_t)}{(1 + k_c)^t} \tag{2}$$

where:

n_t is the number of new company-owned units added in each year, t, through time T, when the firm is assumed to have exhausted all of its growth opportunities.

This model is used in the following section to illustrate how franchising can effect the value of the firm through its effect on the firm's rate of growth.

2.2. GROWTH, VALUE AND FRANCHISING

A numerical example is useful to demonstrate the effect of simply the timing of the firm's growth on the value of the firm. This same example will be used later in the paper to consider the relative profitability of franchise arrangements from the viewpoints of the franchisor and the franchisee.

Assume that each company-owned unit has the following characteristics: annual sales (S_c) are $500,000; costs of production (C_c) are equal to 50 per cent of sales; monitoring costs (m_c) are $40,000 per unit per year; the firm's discount rate (k_c) is 14 per cent; and the investment required to establish a company-owned unit (I) is $500,000. From Equation 1, the net present value of each unit is therefore

$$P_c = \frac{[500(1-0.5)-40]}{0.14} - 500 = \$1 \text{ million}$$

If the firm currently operates ten units, then the value of the existing units is $10 million.

Further assume that the firm knows with certainty that the national market for this product is such that it will support 10,240 units producing and distributing the product. If the firm could instantaneously expand to this level of operations, ceteris paribus, then the net present value of the firm would be $10.24 billion. However, such instantaneous growth is not possible. If the organizational limits on expansion using company-owned units are such that the firm can "only" double its size each year (e.g., so that $N_t = N_0(2^t)$), then it will take the firm ten years to expand to its full market potential of 10,240 units. The path of this expansion is shown as the line AB in Exhibit 1. In the presence of this growth constraint, the value of the firm (V_0 from Equation 2) will be $3.21 billion — considerably less than the $10.24 billion value that would be obtained if the firm could expand instantaneously.

Now consider a situation where franchising enables the firm to grow more rapidly for the organizational reasons discussed earlier (e.g., the substitution of franchisee/owners for managerial employees). Assume that by using a combination of company-owned units and franchisee-owned units, that the firm would be able to triple in size every year rather than only double (i.e., so that $N_t = N_0(3^t)$). At this new rate of expansion, the firm will reach the level of operations that saturates the market (10,240 units) in seven years rather than ten years. This new expansion path is shown as line AC in Exhibit 1. If the present value to the firm of each franchised unit — from the initial franchise fee and subsequent annual royalty payments — is the same

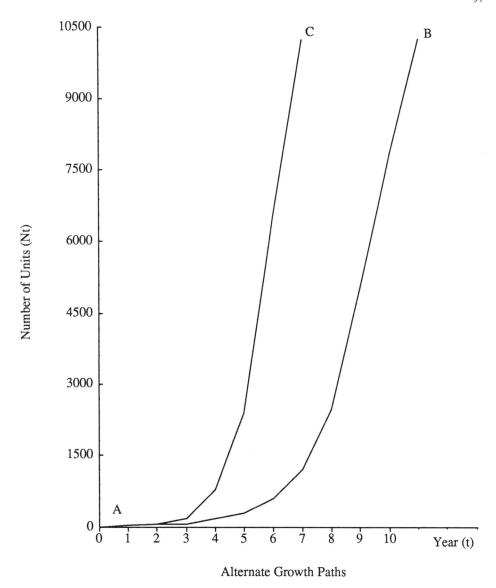

Alternate Growth Paths

Exhibit 1.

as the present value of each company-owned unit ($1 million), then the present value of the firm using the combination of franchisee- and company-owned units would be $4.75 billion, which is 48 per cent higher than the value of $3.21 billion computed for expansion using only company-owned units. This higher value is due solely to the more rapid growth that would be possible using the franchise form of organization.

Our illustration is obviously a hypothetical example, and it depends on the assumption that the present value of a franchisee owned unit to the firm equals that of a company-owned unit — an issue that we consider in the following section. One reason for this assumption was to illustrate the impact on the firm's value of relaxing the growth constraint per se — that is, ignoring any possible differences in the profitability of company-owned versus franchise-owned units. We suggest that one reason why franchising exists as an organizational form is because it permits firms whose products are "franchisable" to grow more rapidly than would otherwise be the case — for reasons that have nothing to due with the acquisition of capital.

3. The Franchise Arrangement

The typical franchise arrangement involves the payment of an initial franchise fee by the franchisee and the periodic payment of a royalty, which is generally a function of the revenue of the franchisee-owned unit.[3] Franchise agreements occasionally include other provisions, such as a requirement that the franchisee purchase certain supplies and materials from the franchisor rather than from outside suppliers. Tying arrangements of this sort are essentially equivalent to a tax on the franchisee's revenue by the franchisor and thus, for simplicity, will not be considered separately in our model (see Caves and Murphy (1976) and Blair and Kasserman (1982)). The financial effects of such provisions are captured in our assumption of a periodic royalty payment. Tying arrangements may also reduce the incidence of "free riding," where franchisees fail to maintain the quality standards required in the franchise agreement (see Klein and Saft (1985)). This free rider problem is a potential agency cost of the franchise arrangement. Although the free rider issue is potentially important in the design of franchise arrangements, it is peripheral to the overall agency motivation for franchising developed below and will therefore be ignored in our subsequent discussion.

In the following sections we use the model developed earlier to analyze the franchising arrangement from the viewpoints of the franchisor and the franchisee, respectively. We show that the benefits of reduced agency costs can be shared between the franchisor and the franchisee, so that the franchise arrangement can be mutually beneficial even in the absence of the growth issue considered above.

3.1. THE FRANCHISOR'S DECISION

The profitability, to the parent company, of a franchisee-owned unit may be denoted as follows:

$$P_f = F + \frac{[a(S_f) - m_f]}{k_c} \tag{3}$$

where:

P_f = net present value of the franchisee-owned unit to the franchisor,
F = initial franchise fee charged to the franchisee,

a = percentage of annual sales used to determine the annual royalty payment,

S_f = annual sales of the franchisee-owned unit,

m_f = annual dollar cost of monitoring the behavior of the franchisee, and

k_c = firm's discount rate.

To simplify the analysis we assume that $S_f = S_c = S$; i.e., that sales per operating unit are the same for franchisee-owned units and company-owned units in our model. Again, recall that for simplicity we also assume that all annual values are perpetuities.

Comparing Equation 3 with Equation 1, we see that, instead of an initial cash outflow by the company (I), the franchisee-owned unit provides an initial cash inflow in the amount of the franchise fee (F). It would appear, however, the subsequent cash flows from the franchisee-owned units will be smaller than from the company-owned units because the franchisor receives only an annual royalty on sales and not the total profits of the unit. That is, in general,

$$S (1 - C_c) - m_c > a (S) - m_f \qquad (4)$$

The percentage annual royalty payment, a, must be set such that the annual profits earned by the franchisee are sufficient to induce him/her to pay the initial franchise fee and to enter into the franchise arrangement. Thus, it is difficult to imagine that Equation 4 would not generally be the case.

There are some important advantages of the franchise form, however, which relate to agency considerations. In particular, the franchise arrangement deals with the incentive problem by making the franchisee a residual claimant, thus probably motivating the franchisee to outperform the manager of a company-owned unit. After all, making an agent a residual claimant and thereby essentially converting him/her into a principal is perhaps the ultimate incentive contract.[4] Even though most managers of company-owned units presumably have sales and profit incentives as a part of their compensation package, the franchise arrangement may provide a superior solution to the incentive problem.

In addition, there is every reason to believe that the costs of monitoring a franchisee-owned unit are considerably less than the costs of monitoring a company-owned unit. The manager of a decentralized company-owned unit must himself be "managed" by the company, and must be further controlled and monitored to reduce shirking, consumption of perquisites, and other agency costs of the sort delineated by Jensen and Meckling (1976). Although the franchisee may have a modest incentive to be less than completely diligent in maintaining the quality of the franchisor's trademark, the level of monitoring required by this problem is probably modest compared to the level of monitoring required for the company-owned units. As one franchisor put it:

... the frequency of district management visits to Franchisor-operated Units is significantly greater than to franchisee-operated Units. (The) Franchisor believes that district management supervision is less critical in the case of a franchisee owner-operator, who should be more directly and personally concerned with the Unit's sanitation, quality and service standards than the employee-manager of a Franchisor-operated unit might be.

These lower monitoring and management costs for franchisee-operated units are, of course, also the primary explanation for the more rapid growth rate associated with the franchise form of organization that were discussed in the preceding section. The firm does not need to expand its management capabilities as much when expansion is through franchising rather than through company-owned units. Thus, the relaxation in the firm's growth constraint also ultimately derives from agency considerations.

The present value — to the franchisor — of a franchisee-owned unit can be computed using Equation 3. Assume that each franchisee-owned unit has the following characteristics: the initial franchise fee (F) is \$500,000; the franchisor charges an annual royalty fee (a) equal to 15 per cent of sales; annual sales for the franchisee-owned units (S) are \$500,000; and annual monitoring costs per unit (m_f) are \$5,000. The value of each franchisee-owned unit, to the franchisor, will be

$$P_f = 500 + \frac{[0.15\,(500) - 5]}{0.14} = \$1 \text{ million}$$

We arbitrarily chose values for our illustration such that the net present value of franchisee-owned units would equal the value of company-owned units ($P_f = P_c$), simply to be consistent with the illustration developed in the preceding section. The franchisor would, of course, wish to extract the maximum profit from the franchisee. In practice, however, the franchisor would also face some important limitations with regard to the setting of the franchise fee and the annual royalty. In particular, these values must be set at a level that will induce large (or, at least, sufficient) numbers of franchisees to enter into the franchise agreement. The market for franchisees appears to be reasonably competitive, which places limits on the franchisor's ability to behave as a monopolist. Franchise arrangements offered by different franchisors are substitutes from the viewpoint of the franchisee. In the following section, we close the loop by considering the franchise arrangement from the viewpoint of the franchisee.

3.2. THE FRANCHISEE'S DECISION

In this section, we assume that a potential franchisee will be willing to enter into the franchise arrangement when the investment has a positive net present value to the franchisee. (Osteryoung (1985) presents some more sophisticated approaches to this decision.) The net present value of a franchisee-owned unit can be denoted as follows:

$$PV = \frac{S\,(1 - C_f - a)}{k_f} - F - 1 \tag{5}$$

where:
C_f = variable cost of production for a franchisee-owned unit expressed as a percentage of sales,
k_f = franchisee's required rate of return, and the other terms are as defined earlier.

We suggest that there will be some important differences between franchisee-owned units and company-owned units. If the franchise agreement greatly reduces certain agency costs, such as shirking and perquisite consumption, by making the franchisee a residual claimant, then presumably the franchisee will perform better than the manager of a company-owned unit. In the context of our model, better performance can be defined as $C_f < C_c$. Based on a study of franchisee-owned and company-managed restaurants, Shelton (1967) presents some fairly impressive empirical evidence that franchisees do in fact outperform company-employed managers in this fashion.

Note that some portion of the higher profitability of franchisee-owned units may be due to contractual shirking by the franchisee (i.e., the so-called "free rider" problem). In particular, the franchisee may have an incentive to cheat on the franchise agreement by, for example, offering a lower quality product than agreed upon. Widespread behavior of this sort would lower the value of the franchisor's trademark. However, franchise agreements are generally closely written and carry substantial penalties for cheating, which reduces both the incentive to cheat and, therefore, the need to monitor (see Klein and Saft (1985)).

The franchisee's investment in a single unit is more risky than the franchisor's geographically diversified holdings of company-owned units and royalty rights from franchised units. Thus, we would expect $k_f > k_c$. The profitability of the franchisee-owned unit need not exceed the profitability of a company-owned unit by enough to offset both this difference in required return and the royalty and franchise fees in order for both the franchisee and the franchisor to benefit from the franchise arrangement, however, because the franchisor also benefits from more rapid growth.

To conclude our numerical example, assume that the franchisee's costs of production (C_f) is equal to 40 per cent of sales (compared to 50 per cent for company-owned units) and that the franchisee's discount rate (k_f) is 20 per cent. The net present value of the unit to the franchisee will therefore be

$$P_v = \frac{500\,(1 - 0.4 - 0.15\,)}{0.20} - 500 - 500 = \$125 \text{ thousand}$$

Thus, the franchise arrangement has a positive net present value from the view point of the franchisee. Our illustration shows that a set of conditions can exist where the franchise agreement is both viable for the franchisee and where the use of franchising increases the value of the franchisor's firm. The force that drives this outcome is the lower agency costs that result from the franchise form of organization.

4. Growth versus Incentives

We have identified two possible reasons for the existence of the franchise form of organization: to enable rapid growth and to reduce agency costs. A number of researchers have suggested that the former factor is the dominant reason for franchising, and that as franchise systems mature we would expect to observe a tendency toward company ownership of all units (see Oxenfeldt and Kelly (1968), Crandall (1970), and Hunt (1973, 1977)). Indeed, some of the papers cited in the preceding sentence reported observing such a trend in the early 1970's. However, more recent data suggest that this trend may have been a temporary phenomenon.

Exhibit 2 shows changes in ownership in franchise businesses for the 11-year period from 1973 through 1983. Although more units were repurchased by franchisors than were converted to franchisee-ownership during 1973 and 1974, since 1975 the reverse has been true. Kostecka (1985, p. 11) makes the following observation about these data:

Since 1975, the trend in franchising has reflected an increase in conversions of company-owned units to franchisee-ownership, and as in previous years the survey shows that most units repurchased for company-ownership were temporary buy-backs for a multitude of reasons, the least of which was the company's desire to withdraw from the franchise system or to operate these units permanently itself.

These data do not indicate that franchisors are engaging in large-scale buybacks of franchisee-owned units in order to convert them to company-owned units.

Exhibit 3 shows the overall ownership structure in franchise businesses for the 1973-1983 period. Although there has been a slight decline in the proportion of franchisee-owned units between 1973 and 1983, from 82.6 per cent in 1973 to 80.9 per cent in 1983 — there is no evidence of a major trend toward company-owned operations. A number of other recent studies have reached this same conclusion (e.g., see Anderson (1984) and Marquardt and Murdock (1986)). The absence of any trend toward company ownership supports the hypothesis that agency considerations are important in explaining the franchise form of organization. In fact, the proportion of franchisee-owned versus company-owned units has been amazingly stable over a long period of time both in the aggregate and at the level of the individual firm. These data suggest that franchisors believe that there is an optimal breakdown between franchisee-owned and company-owned units, in much the same manner that data regarding financial structure suggest that firms believe there is an optimal capital structure. When asked about the existence of an "optimal" franchise structure, Robert B. Ryan, Vice President and Treasurer of McDonald's Corporation, made the following response in correspondence:

> Your observation with regard to the relationship of franchised restaurants to Company operated restaurants is correct.
> McDonald's has found that this relationship produces the best overall results. It provides a large group of aggressive enterprising involved independent businessmen and business women to keep the system green and growing. It also gives the Company a sufficient number of restaurants in diversified areas of the world so that it can experiment, do research and solve problems for the system. Company operated restaurants also provide additional revenue beyond franchising.

In summary, it appears that there may be an optimal franchise structure related to the growth and agency considerations delineated in this paper. The determinants of the optimal franchise structure for a particular franchisor is a fruitful area for further research.

5. Conclusion

We suggest that franchising exists as an organizational form because (1) it permits the franchisor to expand more rapidly than would be possible using only company-owned units and (2) it reduces agency costs that would otherwise be associated with the use of company-employed managers. The latter factor is especially important, and derives from the fact that there are essentially no incentive problems in owner-managed small businesses. The franchisor and the franchisee may be thought of as sharing the benefits arising from these reduced agency costs.

From the viewpoint of public policy toward encouraging the development of small business,

Exhibit 2. Changes In Ownership, 1973 - 1983

Year	Units Repurchased by Company	Unit Converted to Franchisee Ownership
1973	992	659
1974	878	668
1975	716	725
1976	546	956
1977	619	839
1978	612	718
1979	710	1,052
1980	808	1,012
1981	760	1,068
1982	707	1,057
1983	549	1,069

Source: A. Kostecka, Franchising in the Economy 1983-85, U.S. Department of Commerce, January 1985

Exhibit 3. Company-owned versus Franchisee-owned Units, 1973-1983

Year	Percentage of Company-owned Units	Percentage of Franchisee-owned Units
1973	17.4%	82.6%
1974	17.9	82.1
1975	18.5	81.5
1976	18.8	81.2
1977	19.0	81.0
1978	18.7	81.3
1979	18.9	81.1
1980	19.3	80.7
1981	19.4	80.6
1982	19.4	80.6
1983	19.1	80.9

Source: Computed from information in A. Kostecka, Franchising in the Economy 1983-1985, U.S. Department of Commerce, January 1985

franchising may be thought of as enabling society to benefit from the efficiency and productivity of highly motivated owner-managers. Franchising encourages the creation of such businesses by providing the owner-manager with an established product, a proven production process, and training and support in the areas of financial management and marketing. Historically the development of small businesses has been facilitated by government programs such as the Small Business Administration. The evolution of franchising as an organizational form is essentially a free market solution to the problem of providing small business opportunities for potential entrepreneurs.

Endnotes

1. Inaba (1980) conjectures that franchising may be used to extend the monopoly power of the franchisor. However, it is unclear why this goal could not be more easily accomplished through vertical and/or horizontal expansion without franchising.

2. See, also, Mathewson and Winter (1985).

3. Royalty fees are generally specified as a function of sales, rather than profits, presumably because sales figures are less subject to manipulation by the franchisee.

4. Actually, it is not clear that franchisees are owners in the traditional sense. Most franchise arrangements can be terminated by the franchisor for cause, and in many cases the sale of an existing franchise must be approved by the franchisor. Strictly speaking, the incentive effect derived not from ownership per se but, rather, from the fact that franchisees perceive themselves to be owners.

References

Anderson, Evan E. (December 1984) 'The Growth and Performance of Franchise Systems: Company Versus Franchisee Ownership', Journal of Economics and Business 36, 421-431.

Blair, R., and Kasserman, D. (October 1982) 'Optimal Franchising', Southern Economic Journal 48, 494-504.

Brealey, Richard A., and Meyers, Stewart C. (1988) Principles of Corporate Finance, 3rd. edition, McGraw-Hill.

Brickley, James A., and Dark, Frederick H. (June 1987) 'The Choice of Organizational Form: The Case of Franchising', Journal of Financial Economics 18, 401-420.

Caves, Richard E. and Murphy II, William F. (April 1976) 'Franchising: Firms, Markets, and Intangible Assets', Southern Economic Journal 42, 572-586.

Copeland, Thomas E., and Weston, J. Fred (1983) Financial Theory and Corporate Policy, 2nd edition. Addison-wesley.

Crandall, Robert W. (January 1970) 'The Decline of the Franchised Dealer in the Automobile Repair Market', Journal of Business 43, 19-30.

Hunt, Shelby, D. (Summer 1973) 'The Trend Toward Company-operated Units in Franchise Chains', Journal of Retailing 49, 3-12.

Hunt, Shelby D. (Fall 1987) 'Franchising: Promises, Problems, Prospects', Journal of Retailing 53, 71-84.

Inaba, Frederick S. (July 1980) 'Franchising: Monopoly by Contract', Southern Economic Journal 47, 65-72.

Jensen, Michael C. and Meckling, William H. (October 1976) 'Theory of the Firm: Managerial Behavior, Agency Costs and Ownership Structure', Journal of Financial Economics 3, 305-360.

Klein, Benjamin, and Saft, Lester F. (May 1985) 'The Law and Economics of Franchise Tying Contracts', Journal of Law and Economics 28, 345-361.

Kostecka, Andrew (January 1985) Franchising in the Economy 1983-1985, U.S. Department of Commerce.

Marquardt, Raymond A. and Murdock, Gene W. (1986) 'An Evaluation of Franchising Trends and Their Implications to the Retailing Industry', unpublished paper, University of Wyoming.

Mathewson, G. Frank and Winter, Ralph A. (October 1985) 'The Economics of Franchise Contracts', Journal of Law and Economics 28, 503-526.

Osteryoung, Jerome S. (1985) 'A Capital Budgeting Model for the Valuation of a Franchise Agreement', unpublished paper, Florida State University.

Oxenfeldt, Alfred R., and Kelly, Anthony O. (Winter 1968-69) 'Will Successful Franchise Systems Ultimately Become Wholly-owned Chains?', Journal of Retailing 44, 69-83.

Oxenfeldt, Alfred R., and Thompson, Donald N. (Winter 1968-69) 'Franchising in Perspective', Journal of Retailing 44, 3-13.

Penrose, Edith T. (1959) The Theory of the Growth of the Firm, Blackwell.

Rubin, Paul H. (April 1978) 'The Theory of the Firm and the Structure of the Franchise Contract,', Journal of Law and Economics 21, 223-234.

Shelton, John P. (December 1967) 'Allocative Efficiency vs. X-efficiency: Comment', American Economic Review 57, 1252-1258.

OPTIMUM MANAGEMENT CONTRACTING, AGENCY PROBLEM AND THE SIZE OF THE FIRM: A BACKGROUND ANALYSIS

RASSOUL YAZDIPOUR
School of Business
California State University, Fresno
Fresno, CA 93740

MOON H. SONG
School of Business
San Diego State University
San Diego, CA 92182

ABSTRACT. This paper provides some basic ideas toward constructing an alternative framework for settling up the incurrence of agency costs in an enterprise. We first solve for the optimum amount of shirk consumption under the classical and managerial theories of the firm and then extend the analysis to situations where monitoring activities exist.

1. Introduction

Separation of decision making and risk-bearing functions, common among the modern enterprise, and the resultant agency costs created by such structures has troubled financial economists since Berle and Means (1932). Recent breakthrough works by Jensen and Meckling (1976), Fama (1980), Fama and Jensen (1983), Demsetz (1983), and Demsetz and Lehn (1985) have all made great advancements in this important area of financial economics. Demsetz and Lehn (1985, p. 1158) especially argue that:

> "As the value-maximizing size of the firm grows, both the risk neutral and the risk aversion effects of larger size ultimately should weigh more heavily than the shirking cost that may be expected to accompany a more diffuse ownership structure, so that an inverse relationship between firm size and concentration of ownership is to be expected."

The underlying premise of almost all the studies is that the interests of the management (decision agent) do not coincide perfectly with those of the owner (risk-bearer). The implication of this is that the profit maximization objective of the firm will not be necessarily followed and, as a result, corporate resources will be used for other purposes. This is especially true

109

R. Yazdipour (ed.), Advances in Small Business Finance, 109–119.

when the managerial labor market and the market for corporate control can not operate costlessly.

However, recent works on agency problems- including the ones mentioned above- have only provided general solutions and explanations for ownership structure without attempting to provide a quantifiable measure through which a full ex-post settling up can be achieved. Given the absence of such a measure and the lack of a costless market for corporate control and managerial labor, management will go unchecked and unsettled in spending the resources of the firm. This is exactly where the present paper comes in. The objective of this paper is to provide some basic ideas for constructing a framework with potential capabilities in determining optimum ranges of shirk consumption by management and setting the stage for the construction of a comprehensive settlement schedule. Our approach can be viewed as an alternative solution to Fama's (1980) settling up framework. There is no need to make any assumptions about the managerial labor market and the market for corporate control. The authors' views on the above markets are those of Demsetz and Lehn (1985), which treat such mechanisms as costly and restrictive.

Section 2 will briefly talk about the theories of the firm, Section 3 will provide the analysis with taking into account the incurrence of monitoring costs, and finally, section 4 will conclude the paper.

2. The Theories Of The Firm

The theories of the firm can generally be categorized under two headings:

1 - The Classical Theory and
2 - The Managerial Theory

In this section we will only delineate the major differences between these two theories. To start, we should say that under the classical assumption the only reason for incurring any kind of expenditure is its expected contribution to the productivity- profit - of the firm and the entrepreneur is considered to be personally neutral as far as the nature of the expense is concerned: Expense symmetry. However, the situation changes under the managerial theory since "expense preference" is taken into consideration. Managers are no longer neutral at expending the resources of the firm; they care more about some expenses and less about other ones.

Given the self-interest paradigm, the manager certainly wants to spend more on those items that tighten his grip and enhance his control over the firm. One such example is giving top money or quick promotions to the dedicated middle managers who follow the manager's lines. Expending excessive money to resist value-increasing take-overs is another example. Beside these "side payments" to others - which are really payments to the manager himself - costs will also be incurred for the manager's own personal consumption. Examples are "business travels", large offices, private use of the company's facilities, etc. All of the above outlays (direct or indirect) can be thought of as some form of non-pecuniary income for the manager. These costs are non-existent under the classical assumption where the owner's best interest is the main concern. However, they play a major role in the behavior of firms in today's world which is the main concern of this paper.

3. The Analysis

To forward the analysis, variables are defined and assumptions are stated as follows:

The Variables
P = total profit of the firm
R = total revenue of the firm: price times quantity
C = total cost of production; management costs excluded
K = salary of management: pecuniary rewards
S = that part of the firm's resources (inputs) expended under management's discretion and wish: Non-pecuniary consumption (income) by the manager. This is the main variable to be solved for in this paper. Here, S can be thought of as "staff" and "emoluments" as in Williamson (1967), or any other type of perk in general. The major point is that these are the firm's resources expended by the manager the way he/she likes best, or the way he/she gets the highest satisfaction. This again means such resources are not necessarily spent because they are productive to the firm.
M = total cost of managing the firm. M = S + K.

The Assumptions
1. Managers draw satisfaction from two sources:
   a - Pecuniary gain (such as salary): K
   b - Non-pecuniary gain: S; and the utility function[1], therefore, is:

$$U = U (K,S). \tag{1}$$

2. Manager's reward function can be shown as:

$$W = K + Z (S) \tag{2}$$

where, Z(S) is the manager's subjective "satisfaction function[2]" which is a function of S and can be expressed in dollar terms. Z is assumed to be an increasing function of S, but at a decreasing rate.

3. Finally, consumption of one unit of S decreases firm's value by one dollar.

We can now write our two objective functions as follows:

$$Max P = R - C - M \tag{3}$$
$$Max U = U (K,S). \tag{4}$$

The first is the objective function if we accept the "shareholders' best interest hypothesis" as in the classic theory where there is perfect competition for all kinds of input- including the managerial labor input. The second is the objective function if the "manager's best interest hypothesis" is accepted in the managerial theory.

3.1. THE SHAREHOLDERS' BEST INTEREST HYPOTHESIS

If we assume the manager's goal as one of maximizing the shareholders wealth, then we can use the standard maximization technique to solve - among other things - for the optimum amount of S: The non-pecuniary consumption by the manager of the firm's resources:

$$
\begin{aligned}
P &= R - [C + M] \\
&= R - [C + K + S] \\
&= R - [C + (W - Z(S)) + S].
\end{aligned}
$$

We now solve for the optimum amount of S: S^* here.

$$\frac{\partial P}{\partial S} = \frac{\partial Z(S)}{\partial S} - 1 = 0$$

$$\frac{\partial Z(S)}{\partial S} = 1 \quad \text{or} \quad Z'(S) = 1 \tag{5}$$

This is the familiar classical condition of equality of marginal benefit (satisfaction here) and marginal cost. For example, if we refer to S as "staff" (like the selling and administrative staff), this condition tells us: Expand staff until the marginal benefit of the last "unit" of staff is equal to one dollar - its marginal cost. Figure 1 depicts one such relationship.

From (5):

$$S^* = Z'^{-1}(1) \tag{6}$$

S^* is the optimum amount of perk usage from the management's - here also the entrepreneur's or owner-manager's - point of view and sets the lower limit in a series of S as we move from the classical assumption of perfect markets and the "oneness" of ownership and management toward the paradigm of imperfect markets and total separation of management and ownership under the managerial theory of the firm.

This lower level S^* can be compared to the Jensen-Meckling's F-level at zero value. In other words, at S^* the value of the firm is at its maximum and the entrepreneur owns 100 percent of the firm ($\alpha = 100\%$).

3.2. THE MANAGER'S BEST INTEREST HYPOTHESIS

With management's interest as the main concern, the objective function then becomes:

$$
\begin{aligned}
&\text{Max } U = U(K,S) \\
&\text{subject to: } K + Z(S) = W.
\end{aligned} \tag{7}
$$

This is a constrained maximization problem to be solved for. However; before going through the solution it may be useful to look into the following relationships as shown in Figure 2.

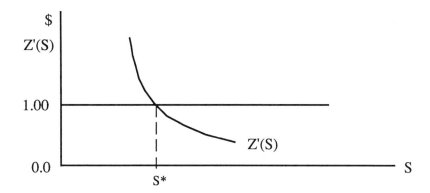

Figure 1. Optimum amount of perk consumption under the Classical Theory.

In Figure 2, point S* is the same as in Figure 1 in the previous section: It is the profit-maximizing solution with its corresponding α equal to unity (α is the portion of the firm held by the owner-manager). However, in this section we want to see how far S will travel away from its initial position of S* and where it will settle down as the entrepreneur sells some (1-α) portion of her ownership to outside equity holders.

First of all, if she keeps an interest equal to α in the firm, then her marginal cost (MC) is only: α x $1 = $α < 1. Therefore, she has an incentive to consume more S. Secondly, she will only increase her consumption of S up to the point S** in the figure. Beyond that point, marginal benefit (MB) is less than the marginal cost. This S**, where at that point MB = MC, sets the upper limit in the range mentioned in the previous section. Again, if S is referred to as "staff", S** is the number of "units" of staff that maximizes the manager's utility function. For points below S** the ratio between MB and MC is not equal to one anymore as was the case under the classical setting: It is -as can be seen from the figure 2 - less than one and the manager expands staff, for example, beyond its classical optimum level.

Now let us go back to equation 7 and push the analysis a bit forward. Setting the Lagrangian as follows and taking the partial derivative of L with respect to K, S and λ respectively will produce:

$$L = U(K,S) + \lambda [W - K - Z(S)] \qquad (8)$$

$$\frac{\partial L}{\partial K} = U_k - \lambda = 0 \qquad (9)$$

$$\frac{\partial L}{\partial S} = U_s - \lambda\, Z'(S) = 0 \tag{10}$$

$$\frac{\partial L}{\partial \lambda} = W - K - Z(S) = 0. \tag{11}$$

From (9) and (10):

$$\frac{U_s}{U_k} = Z'(S) \tag{12}$$

Note that λ is the marginal utility of the total compensation (W). Given equation 12 and figure 2, the following statements can be made:

1. At point S^*, $Z'(S) = 1$ and therefore, $U_s = U_k$; and there is no incentive for more consumption of S beyond S^*. This is the classical setting: Entrepreneurial firm.
2. For the range located between the S^*-S^{**} region which is our main area of concern, we have:

$$1 > \frac{U_s}{U_k} > \alpha \quad \text{and} \quad MB > MC$$

which means more consumption of S up to S^{**}.

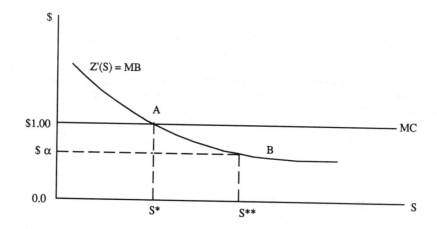

Figure 2. The upper- and lower-limits on shirk consumption

At S**:

$$\frac{U_s}{U_k} = \alpha \quad \text{and} \quad MB = MC$$

which is the optimum point as far as the owner-manager is concerned. As stated previously, the owner-manager's actual location on the S-axis, as compared to S* and S**, determines her degree of loyalty toward other shareholders.

In other words, managerial loyalty will be a function of:

$$\frac{S^{**} - S^*}{S^*} .$$

To better visualize this concept, it would be useful if we take the inverse of such a product:

$$\frac{1}{\dfrac{S^{**} - S^*}{S^*}}$$

This product can now be referred as the "Degree of Managerial Loyalty" (DML). When the entrepreneur is also the manager of her company, her "degree of managerial loyalty" is infinite.

3. For the points beyond S**:

$$\frac{U_s}{U_k} < \alpha \quad \text{and} \quad MB < MC$$

and therefore, there is no incentive for consuming more perk beyond that point.

To summarize, by plugging in different levels of managerial ownership (α) the optimum level of shirk consumption by management can be calculated. Such an optimum level can be used as the basis for putting together a market-value maximizing compensation package for managers.

3.3. ANALYSIS WITH THE EXISTENCE OF MONITORING ACTIVITIES

Let:
1) C = C(N). N is monitoring activity and C(N) is a monitoring cost function.

$$\frac{\partial C}{\partial N} > 0 \quad \text{and} \quad \frac{\partial^2 C}{\partial^2 N} > 0$$

2) S = S (N). S(N) is a perk-consumption function.

$$\frac{\partial S}{\partial N} < 0 \quad \text{and} \quad \frac{\partial^2 S}{\partial^2 N} > 0 .$$

The two functions can be represented as shown in Figure 3. As can be seen from the graph, there is an optimum level of monitoring activity that minimizes the sum of the monitoring costs and perk consumption costs. Note that a given level of α should be specified for any such analysis. Also note the vertical intercept has been marked as $s_{\alpha_1}^{**}$, which is comparable to s^{**} in Figure 2 - s^{**} is the manager's optimum shirk consumption when there is no monitoring activity.

The change in α shifts the S(N) function accordingly. If the entrepreneur holds a larger proportion of the company (high α), he/she has to bear more of the monitoring costs. The following Figure 4 graphs the same functions for two different levels of α. Given Figure 3 or 4, if the owner(s) bears the optimum level of monitoring costs (related to the optimum level of monitoring activity at $N_{\alpha_1}^*$), then an upper limit of shirk consumption such as $s_{N^*}^{\alpha_1}$ can be set by shareholders.

4. Summary And Conclusion

As of today, and as far as is known, there does not exist a cost-effective control procedure to be used as a tool in satisfactorily resolving the agency problems in the modern enterprise - the managerial labor market and the market for corporate control being exemptions. The management goes unchecked as to its loyalty and conformity toward the interests of the risk-

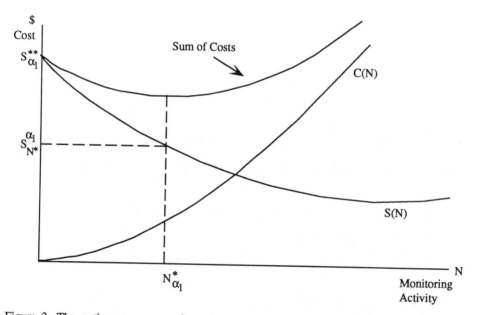

Figure 3. The optimum amount of monitoring given the perk-consumption and monitoring cost function

bearers. The need for the development of such a tool has been the driving force behind the attempt made in this paper.

The authors have provided some basic ideas toward constructing an alternative framework for resolving and settling up the agency issues created in the modern enterprise. The relationships discussed in the paper can provide varying ranges of optimum shirk consumption by the owner-manager; as a function of the percentage of ownership held in the company. Monitoring consideration has also been included in the analysis. Once the parameters of the model are determined, and given the fact that the total managerial compensation (salary plus shirk) across similar companies are the same, an ex-post settling up can be achieved.

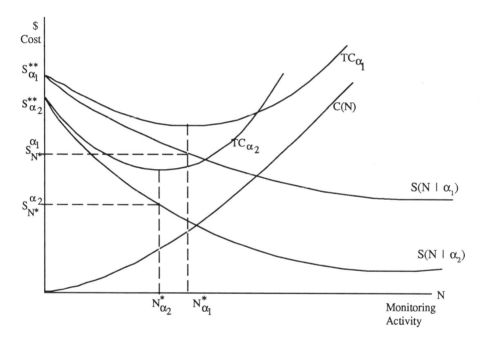

Figure 4. Optimum monitoring activities for two levels of management ownership.
Note, $\alpha1 < \alpha2$

Endnotes

1. Utility is assumed to be a concave function of shirk consumption and salary: $U' > 0$, $U'' < 0$.

2. Knober (1986) [10] argues for a similar satisfaction function.

References

Alchian, A. and Demsetz, H. (1972) 'Production, Information Costs and Economic Organization', American Economic Review, v.62, 777-795.

Berle, A. and Means G. (1932) 'The Modern Corporation and Private Property', Macmillan.

Cyret, R.M. and March, J.G. (1963) 'A Behavioral Theory of the Firm', Prentice-Hall, Inc., Englewood Cliffs, N.J..

Demsetz, H. (1983) 'The Structure Of Ownership and the Theory of the Firm', Journal of Law and Economics, v.91, 375-393

Demsetz H. and Lehn K. (1985) 'The Structure of Corporate Ownership: Causes and Consequences', Journal of Political Economy, v.93, 1155-1177.

Fama, E.F. (1980) 'Agency Problems and the Theory of the Firm', Journal of Political Economy, v.88, 288-307.

Fama E. F. and Jensen M. (1983) 'Separation of Ownership and Control', Journal of Law and Economics, v.26, 301-325.

Fama E. F. and Jensen M. (1983) 'Agency Problem and Residual Claim', Journal of Law and Economics, v.26, 327-349.

Jensen, M.C. and Meckling, W.H. (1976) 'Theory of the Firm: Managerial Behavior, Agency Costs and Ownership Structure', Journal of Financial Economics, v.11, 5-50.

Knober, C.R. (1986) 'Golden Parachutes, Shark Repellents, and Hostile Tender Offers', American Economic Review, v.76, 155-167.

Wildsmith, J.R. (1973) 'Managerial Theories of the Firm', Martin Robertson and Co. Ltd., London.

Williamson, O.E. (1967) 'The Economics of Discretionary Behavior: Managerial Objectives in a Theory of the Firm', Markham Publishing Co., Chicago.

RISK AND RETURN IN SMALL BUSINESS LENDING: THE CASE OF COMMERCIAL BANKS

ANDREW J. BUCK
Department of Economics
School of Business and Management
Temple University
Philadelphia, PA 19122

JOSEPH FRIEDMAN
Department of Finance
School of Business and Management
Temple University
Philadelphia, PA 19122

WILLIAM C. DUNKELBERG
National Federation of Independent Business and,
Dean, School of Business and Management
Temple University
Philadelphia, PA 19122

ABSTRACT. The paper proposes a framework for modeling the risk-return tradeoff faced by institutions lending to small firms. A loan contract is viewed as a vector of several negotiable attributes including the interest rate to be paid, the term of loan, the size of both the loan and collateral, and the rate at which the loan to be repaid. A model of the loan contracting process is outlined. Then some "stylized" facts about the relation between small businesses and their banks are presented. Empirical models of the loan granting decision and of the determinants of the interest margin paid by small firms is estimated.

1. Introduction

Economists have been puzzled by the existence of credit rationing for several decades. Baltensperger (1978) and Baltensperger and Devinney (1985) review a literature that begins with Kareken (1957) and Hodgman (1960). The earliest papers in the genre had attempted a neo-classical explanation of a seeming failure of the market to achieve a Walrasian equilibrium. More recent efforts, reviewed, in part, in Stiglitz (1987), have introduced notions of adverse selection, moral hazard, asymmetric risk assessment by borrower and lender and monitoring costs as explanations for what is termed credit rationing.

121

R. Yazdipour (ed.), Advances in Small Business Finance, 121–137.

A loan contract has a number of negotiable facets, including the interest rate to be paid, the term of loan, the size of both the loan and collateral, and the rate at which the loan is to be repaid. Consideration of these features is presented in Plaut (1985). In his model a change in loan size changes the loan package and the results in a different product. For given rate of repayment, interest, term and amount of collateral, there is a maximum loan size that will be offered to borrowers. In this framework it is quite likely that potential borrowers could present loan requests whose terms are consistent only with immediate repayment or 100% liquid collateral. Under such conditions the loan request is denied.

Plaut and Melnick (1986) have tried to operationalize some of these concepts using survey data for 101 U.S. nonfinancial firms. However, their data had so few explanatory variables that they were able to draw only a few substantive conclusions.

The present paper is first in a series of papers trying to assess the consequences of bankruptcy reform (Scott and Smith(1986)), high inflation rates and bank deregulation, on lending to small firms. The paper proposes an appropriate framework for modeling the risk-return tradeoff faced by institutions lending to small firms. The structure of the essay is as follows: Section two outlines a model of the loan contracting process. Section three provides some 'stylized' facts about the relation between small businesses and their banks. The empirical model is presented in section four. The paper closes with conclusions and recommendations for future work.

2. Loan Contracts and Rationing

A loan contract is a two party agreement that involves negotiation along a number of dimensions. While the process may, in reality, involve a dynamic negotiation, we consider a simpler take-it-or-leave-it framework that contains all the essential terms of a loan contract. For a given risk assessment of the applicant by the lender, there are a set of terms which the bank is prepared to offer. Given the applicants assessment of the riskiness of his project, he may or may not accept those terms. This failure to achieve overlapping offer sets produces the phenomenon characterized as "rationing."

The loan contract consists of six major terms: The size of the loan, L_0; the rate of repayment, d; the net application fee, K; the interest rate, r; the term of the loan, T; and the requisite collateral, C.

2.1. THE LENDER

Once the interest rate and rate of repayment have been established, the outstanding amount of the loan at any point in time is

$$L_t = L_0 \cdot e^{(r-\delta)t} \tag{2.1}$$

If the borrower repays δ of the outstanding balance each period, then the present value of the periodic payment, discounted at the an opportunity rate ρ, is

$$\delta L_0 \cdot e^{(r-\rho-\delta)t} \tag{2.2}$$

The present value of the final payment to the bank will be in the amount of

$$[L_0 \cdot e^{(r-\rho-\delta)T}] - 1 \tag{2.3}$$

The bank also receives an application or origination fee, K_0. The cost of acquiring information and processing the application, $K(\theta)$, is subtracted from K_0. The acquisition of information allows the lender to sharpen its prior on the likelihood of applicant's default. Assuming that additional information θ becomes increasingly expensive,

$$K'(\theta) < 0 \text{ and } K''(\theta) > 0$$

If the borrower does not default on the loan, the bank's profit over the life of the loan, Π_N, is the sum of the integral of (2.2) over the life of the loan, the final payment (2.3) and net fees, $K(\theta) = K_0 - K(\theta)$:

$$\Pi_N = L_0 \cdot \left[1 + \frac{\delta}{(r - \rho - \delta)} \right] \cdot [e^{(r - \rho - \delta)T} - 1] + K(\theta) \tag{2.4}$$

If the borrower defaults at time t the bank will have received the net fee, the periodic payments through t, plus the present value of the collateral, less the outstanding balance of the loan. Thus, in the event of default, the bank's profit is

$$\Pi_D(t) = L_0 \cdot \left[1 + \frac{\delta}{(r - \rho - \delta)} \right] \cdot [e^{(r - \rho - \delta)t} - 1] + K(\theta) + C \cdot e^{-\rho t}$$
$$- L_0 \cdot e^{(r - \rho - \delta)t} \tag{2.5}$$

The default probability is a continuous random variant of the geometric probability distribution. Let $\beta(\theta)$ be the bank's prior for the probability of borrower default in any short interval, conditional on the information purchased, θ. It is assumed that the borrower knows the true value of β. The probability of default not occurring until period t is given by

$$\int_0^t \beta(\theta) e^{-\beta(\theta)s} ds$$

and the probability of no default through the end of the loan is given by

$$e^{-\beta(\theta)T}$$

Combining (2.4) and (2.5) with the conditional probability distribution gives an expected profit to the lender:

$$e^{-\beta(\theta)T} \cdot \Pi_N + \int_0^T \beta(\theta) e^{-\beta(\theta)t} \cdot \Pi_D(t) dt \tag{2.6}$$

The problem of the maximization of (2.6) is complicated by the presence and role of θ. To explicate the bank's problem, consider the following discrete case analog. The lending institution has N loans under consideration. Without the purchase of any information the banker would assign to all loans the same probability of default using the historical average default rate. This, however, would not be a desireable business strategy since loans are not homogeneous and the lender has only a finite portfolio.[1]

By purchasing the first level of information, θ_0, the lender can identify the N_0 applicants with the lowest default probability β_0. With the purchase of the next level of information, θ_1, the remaining pool can be further divided. $\alpha(N - N_0)$ applicants would be rated as having default probability β_1, $\beta_2 > \beta_0$, and $(1 - \alpha)(N - N_0)$ would remain in the higher risk pool. The next level of information, θ_2, allows the lender to assign default probability β_2 to $\alpha(1 - \alpha)(N - N_0)$ applicants and $(1 - \alpha)^2(N - N_0)$ applicants would remain in the higher risk pool. In the limit only one applicant would receive this highest probability of default rating.[2] Therefore, it is necessary to integrate out q up to the optimal choice.

The lender's optimization problem involves the choice of θ, r, δ, T, L_0, C and K_0 to make

$$E\Pi^N = \int_0^\theta \left\{ e^{-\beta(\theta)T} \cdot \Pi_N + \int_0^T \beta(\theta)e^{-\beta(\theta)t} \cdot \Pi_D(t)dt \right\} d\theta \tag{2.7}$$

equal to zero for the last borrower. In a competitive loan market the bank's marginal customer should, on average, yield zero cconomic profit.

To determine how the bank adjusts the terms of the loan to yield the optimal contract, we take the total differential of $E\Pi^N$. The signs of the requisite partials are:

$$\psi_1 = \left(\frac{\partial E\Pi_L}{\partial \theta} \right) > 0$$

Since θ improves the lender's judgment of the true probability of default it can increase expected profit. But information becomes increasingly costly, so $E\Pi(\theta)$ will be hump shaped.

$$< 0$$

$$\psi_2 = \left(\frac{\partial E\Pi_L}{\partial r} \right) > 0$$

will be true over all relevant values of r.

$$\psi_3 = \left(\frac{\partial E\Pi_L}{\partial \delta} \right) > 0$$

but goes to zero as $\delta \to \infty$. With instantaneous pay back the lender earns no return. The presumption is that initial fees just cover processing costs.

$$\psi_4 = \left(\frac{\partial E\Pi_L}{\partial T} \right) > 0$$

will be greater than zero as long as the contract length is below some T^*, which is determined by the present value of a future dollar.

$$\psi_5 = \left(\frac{\partial E\Pi_L}{\partial L_0} \right) < 0$$

because of the increase in loss when default occurs. This derivative becomes more negative as L_0 gets large.

$$\psi_6 = \left(\frac{\partial E\Pi_L}{\partial K_0} \right) > 0$$

since the origination fees are paid up front

$$\psi_7 = \left(\frac{\partial E\Pi_L}{\partial C} \right) > 0$$

since a larger collateral reduces losses to the lender in the event of default.

Application of the implicit function theorem to ψ_2 and ψ_3 allows drawing the lenders iso-profit curve for zero expected profit in the r, L_0 plane. This curve will be increasing at an increasing rate. We will return to this after consideration of the borrower.

2.2. THE BORROWER

Let $R_t = R_t(L_0)$ denote the borrower's earnings before interest and debt service. R_t is a function of the loan, L_0, which affects the type and size of projects the borrower can undertake. The present value of earnings from the borrower's project when there is no default is given by

$$\int_0^T R_t e^{-\rho t} dt$$

Allowing for the loan origination fee and debt service, the borrower's profit if he does not default on the loan is

$$\Pi_N^B = \int_0^T R_t \, e^{-\rho t} dt - L_0 \cdot \left[\frac{\delta}{(r-\rho-\delta)} + 1 \right] \cdot [\, e^{(r-\rho-\delta)T} - 1 \,] - K_0$$

In case of default at time t, the borrower forfeits the loan payments already made, the loan origination fee, his collateral, and any retained earnings from the project to time t. The losses in default are:

$$\Pi_D^B = -\int_0^t R_t \, e^{-\rho t} dt - L_0 \cdot \left[\frac{\delta}{(r-\rho-\delta)} + 1 \right] \cdot [\, e^{(r-\rho-\delta)T} - 1 \,] - K_0$$

combining $\Pi_N{}^B$ and $\Pi_D{}^B$ with the probability of no default and default one gets the expected (2.8) profit to the borrower of a particular loan contract:

$$E\Pi^B = e^{-\beta T} \cdot \Pi_N + \int_0^T \beta e^{-\beta} \cdot \Pi_D(t) dt$$

The borrower maximizes $E\Pi_B$ by his choice of L_0, T, r, δ. The fee, K_0 is not part of his optimization problem since it is determined in the bank's competitive market place.[4] Nor does the borrower have any control over θ, the amount of information purchased by the lender. The final difference between the borrower's objective function and the lender's objective function is the role of β, the probability of default in any short time interval. Presumably the borrower knows its true probability of default; or could not sharpen its prior with the acquisition of more information. At the very least it has better information than their lender.

While the borrower is interested in maximizing (2.8), our interest is restricted to the expected profit curve which may be termed the borrower's reservation curve. It is that set of r, L pairs which just give the borrower a zero expected return at the market discount rate. To find this curve equation (2.8) is set to zero and totally differentiated.

The requisite partials are:

$$\Omega_1 = \left(\frac{\partial E\Pi_B}{\partial L_0} \right) > 0 \qquad$$
since profits are increasing in L_0, but $E\Pi$ is decreasing in L_0 when there is default, so Ω_1 approaches zero.

126

$$\Omega_2 = \left(\frac{\partial E\Pi_B}{\partial r} \right) < 0$$

since expected returns diminish with debt service.

$$\Omega_3 = \left(\frac{\partial E\Pi_B}{\partial \delta} \right) < 0$$

since the borrower does not have use of the loan as the repayment rate increases.

$$\Omega_4 = \left(\frac{\partial E\Pi_B}{\partial \delta} \right) > 0$$

since the borrower would prefer not to repay.

Using Ω_1, Ω_2 and the implicit function theorem, the borrower's expected iso-profit curves in the r, L plane will be increasing at a decreasing rate. There is, however, a reservation expected iso-profit curve "below" which the borrower will not go. Such a "lower bound" would require loan agreement terms which would make it more profitable for the borrower to become a lender at the risk free rate.

Figure 1a combines the lender's zero expected iso-profit curve, L*, with the borrower's reservation iso-profit curve, B*.

For the lender the direction of increasing profit is to the northwest. The borrower's direction of increasing profit is to the southeast. The lender is constrained to operating on L* due to the competitive market assumption. Because no assumption has been made about the structure of the market in which the borrower sells his goods, he can try to get a loan that moves him to a higher expected iso-profit curve in the southeast direction. In this panel there are no combinations of loan terms which are agreeable to both parties. In fact, the borrower pictured will not be able to obtain a loan from any of the identical banks in the homogeneous competitive market.

Figure 1b shows the situation where the borrower is able to do better than his reservation expected iso-profit curve. The borrower goes away a happy customer of the bank since he would have been willing to pay as much as $\hat{r}$ for the loan he received, or take a loan of as little as $\hat{L}$ at his contractual interest rate r_0.

If loan contracts and the associated collateral were perfectly fungible, i.e. there were secondary markets in loans, then there would be a market curve in the r, L plane. This is shown as M* in panel 1c. Even though the lender and the borrower do not agree directly on the terms of the loan, they do trade along the market curve so that all offered funds are lent, and all loan requests would be filled. We can use this panel to represent unsatisfied customers of the bank. The borrower would like to have the amount L_0. The bank offers him L_2 at a lower rate. The borrower reports that not all his credit needs are met by his principal bank. The remainder of his needs are met from other sources, perhaps at higher interest rates than his bank loan.

In conclusion, our model is flexible enough to encompass both satisfied and dissatisfied bank customers. It also demonstrates the need for complete secondary markets in business loans. At present these markets are quite limited. The securitization of bank loans is done only for large low risk enterprises. The terms of such securitizations probably do not lower interest rates to borrowers, although they do improve lender's liquidity and spread risk. In any case, there are no such markets for individual or packages of small business loans.

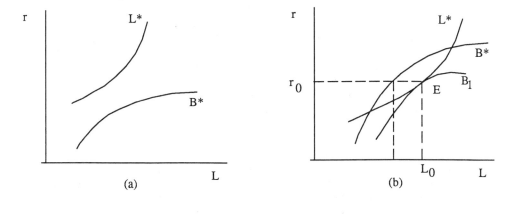

(a)

(b)

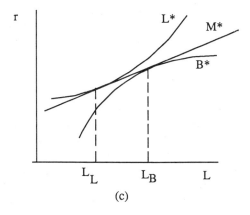

(c)

Figure 1

3. An Assessment of Evidence of Rationing.

The data used in this study are drawn from the third in a series of cross sectional surveys of membership of the National Federation of Independent Businesses (NFIB). The Federation consists of over 500,000 member firms. Small businesses produce about 40% of the private GNP and employ about half the private non-farm workforce. Dunkelberg and Scott (1983) have shown the NFIB membership fairly represents the small business universe. A random sample was drawn from the membership file for the purpose of the survey.[5]

Figure 2 shows the "term structure of interest rates characterizing small business loans. The horizontal axis shows the date of loan origination and the vertical axis shows interest rate paid. The respondents were grouped into short term (less than 12 months), medium term (13 to 60 months), and long term (more than 60 months) loan categories. Surveys were conducted in 1980, 1983 and 1985 producing three distinct sets of yield curves. The 1980 survey shows that the term structure was fairly tight, but that long term loans paid the lowest rates. Similarly, the 1982 term structure curves reflect the very high rates of inflation of the early eighties. The short term borrowers paid a substantial premium to insure the lender against virtually certain inflation loss. The final survey, conducted in 1985 and used in our analysis, shows a very confused term structure. While the economy was in a substantial recovery, there was generally a great deal of uncertainty about the future course of the economy, interest rates and inflation. Inflation was falling, but real credit demands were putting pressure on real credit costs.

Table 1 presents figures for business borrowing which illustrate the extent of rationing and dissatisfaction with loan terms. The data are for three surveys conducted in 1980, 1982 and 1984. Regardless of age, vigor of the business, or state of the economy, significant numbers of firms are being denied loans. Anywhere from 6 to 22% of small businesses are being denied loans, although the fraction of denials has declined with economic recovery. More important than outright denial is the significance of the extent of rationing individual borrowers. For any age of firm, vigor of the business, or year, a significant fraction of borrowers report that not all their credit needs are met. Unlike the figures for denials, there is no discernible pattern in the credit needs' responses.

Failure to obtain all of one's credit needs invariably leads to dissatisfaction with the loan contract. The NFIB members were asked to identify those features of the loan contract which caused the greatest dissatisfaction. The contractual interest rate is always the greatest concern, and the proportion citing interest rates as a problem increases with the real rate of interest.[6] It is interesting to note that only in the 1980 survey were large numbers of firms perturbed by the size of their loan (too small) and its maturity (too short). At that time the Chairman of the Federal Reserve, Mr. Paul Volker, was in the middle of a determined fight against inflation. This suggests an easing of credit availability in later years. However, it appears that lenders remained wary of default though the 1982 survey; collateral requirements were apparently no longer a concern by 1984.

4. Statistical Characterization of Risk and Return.

In this section we use the NFIB data base to identify the lenders' zero expected iso-profit curve when they face small businesses. Bank lending markets are thought to be fairly competitive and, within size class, the lending institutions are similar to one another. Therefore they will share a common expected iso-profit curve. Borrowers, on the other hand, are heterogeneous

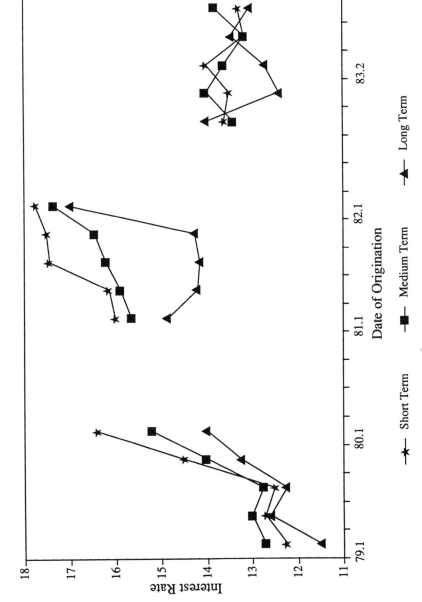

Small Business Loan Yield Curve

Figure 2.

130

TABLE 1. Proportion of firms responding in the affirmative

| | Last Loan Application Rejected | | | Not all Credit Needs Met | | | Reason for Loan Contract Dissatisfaction | | | | | | | | | | | |
| | | | | | | | Interest Rate | | | Amount | | | Maturity | | | Collateral | | |
Years in Business	1980	1982	1984	1980	1982	1984	1980	1982	1984	1980	1982	1984	1980	1982	1984	1980	1982	1984
1-2	21	22	15	56	63	57	42	49	60	11	10	5	11	6	5	10	14	10
3-4	20	21	12	53	61	53	45	54	61	13	9	-	10	5	-	14	12	4
5-6	18	12	12	60	56	50	39	60	70	13	4	-	11	7	-	14	14	-
7-10	13	12	12	50	48	44	45	63	67	10	7	2	10	6	-	18	12	4
11-15	12	10	9	45	49	53	54	69	63	11	5	3	6	3	4	11	10	-
16-20	9	12	11	41	48	45	63	76	81	6	-	-	6	5	5	12	8	5
21+	7	6	6	32	44	43	53	67	73	8	4	-	11	9	2	11	9	2
Business Activity																		
Growing 21+%/year	14	15	13	46	52	47	42	64	73	11	5	3	9	6	-	14	10	3
Growing 6-20%	11	7	10	42	46	46	49	62	65	9	6	-	10	4	2	12	12	2
Steady	10	10	9	38	51	42	50	70	69	10	3	-	11	7	2	12	10	4
Decline	19	12	9	62	52	54	51	63	70	12	6	4	9	7	2	14	12	4
All Firms	13	11	10	-	-	-	49	63	68	10	6	1	10	6	2	13	11	3

and will have different reservation iso-profit curves. Each borrower will be tangent to the lenders' common iso-profit curve. By observing enough borrowers we can construct the lender's iso-profit curve.

The discussions in the previous sections suggest that a loan to a small business can be described as a package of attributes such as the interest rate, the size of the loan, the terms of repayment and collateralization. The decision to seek and the decision to grant the loan both depend on the agents' assessment of the likelihood of default. In formulating this prior bank and the borrower rely on easily observed, verifiable firm attributes such as type of business, size, years in business and owner's equity. However, the agreed upon terms of the contract may not have satisfied the desires of the borrower. Thus, the interest rate paid by a small business may be written as:

$$r_i = \alpha + C_i\beta_i + B_i\beta_2 + \beta_3\left(\frac{D}{E}\right)_i + \text{other variables} + \varepsilon_i \tag{4.1}$$

where: r is the interest rate, C is a vector of dummy variables used to indicate the type of collateral required, B is a vector which characterized the terms of repayment, (D/E) is the debt equity ratio of the borrower, ε is an error term.

There are two problems with estimating the parameters of equation (1), both stemming from sample selection bias. First, for the reasons enumerated above, not all loan applications result in a loan being made. Thus (4.1) is conditional on the applicant being successful. Secondly, the terms of the contract are endogenous to the loan process, whereas in (4.1) they have been treated as exogenous.

To deal with the first type of selection bias we will estimate a probit function that will relate the probability of loan denial to variables describing the bank and the firm. The estimated functions will be used to calculate Heckman's lambda for each observed loan. These lambda are then used as additional explanatory variables in (4.1) (for an explanation of this method see Heckman (1974) and the appendix). In addition to screening out risky loans, a bank can alter the risk-return tradeoff of a loan by requiring the borrower to post collateral. An important question to be answered is whether or not collateral reduces the interest rate paid by the borrower, or merely insures the lender against loss. We address this issue by modifying (4.1) to include a dummy variable that indicates whether collateral was posted.

The NFIB surveys contain little explicit information on origination fees. Consequently, a dummy variable was used to denote the presence of such fees.

Estimated probit functions of the probability that the most recent loan requested has been approved are shown in Table 2. Business age (BAGE) is positively and significantly related to the loan approval probability indicating that young businesses have a higher likelihood of loan denial than do mature businesses. High debt equity ratio (D/E) reduces the likelihood of loan approval, but its effect is non-linear. When D/E is entered linearly (Model A), the effect is negative but significant only at the 15% level. In model B we allowed for a threshold effect by replacing D/E with two dummy variables, DE25L which equals 1 if debt equity ratio is 25% or less, zero otherwise, and DE65P which equals 1 if the debt/equity ratio is 65% or higher, zero otherwise. DE65P is negative and statistically significant, indicating that above the 65% debt/equity threshold the probability of loan denial increases. The type of business organization (proprietorship, partnership or corporation) did not affect loan approval probabilities, nor is there any important industry effect. It is worth noting, however, that the probability of loan approval is smaller if the application was made at a large bank.

TABLE 2. Estimated Probit Function: Loan Application Approved
(Standard Errors in Parentheses)

	Model A	Model B
Intercept	2.7061	2.6248
	(0.3831)	(0.3445)
Proprietor	-.2398	-.2829
	(0.2287)	(0.2117)
Partnership	-.2843	-.2944
	(0.3809)	(0.3493)
Large Bank	-.7386	-.7747
	(0.2042)**	(0.1895)**
Manufacturing/Mining	-.5793	-.5120
	(.3790)	(.3525)
Transportation	.5771	.5051
	(.5935)	(.5332)
Retail/Wholesale	-.4745	-.4678
	(.3345)	(.3050)
Agriculture	.3357	.0958
	(.5991)	(.5079)
Finance	-.4708	-.4190
	(.4180)	(.3788)
Service	.6158	.6976
	(.5552)	(.5375)
Business age	.0189	.0161
	(.0078)**	(.0071)**
Debt/Equity	-.6016	———
	(.4219)	
DE25L	———	.0999
		(.2083)
DE65P	———	-.5383
		(2.981)**
-2log likelihood		
intercept only	733.69	733.69
at convergence	695.05	690.26
CHI Square (d.f.)	38.64 (11)	43.43 (12)
ROH (ρ)	0.053	0.059

** significant at 1%

* significant at 5%

+ significant at 10%

Next we examine the determinants of the interest rate margin on approved loans. The margin is defined as the difference between the contract interest rate and the prime rate that prevailed at the time the loan was made. Regression estimates of the margin equation are presented in Table 3. Equation A was not corrected for the selection bias, equation B was corrected for selection bias using Heckman's procedure. The discussion here is based on equation B (The coefficient of Heckman's Lambda has no economic interpretation. A significant coefficient indicates that selection bias was present). "Prime Plus" loans are variable rate loans which are specified at the time the loan is granted in terms of the prime rate plus a margin. Such loans are initially cheaper, by .37%, than fixed rate loans. We saw earlier that large banks are more likely than other banks to turn away loan applications of small businesses. It is apparent from Table 3, though, that the successful applicant to a large bank is rewarded with a less expensive loan. Large banks interest rate margins are smaller by .45% than those of other banks.. Business age does not matter in determining margins, once the selection bias is corrected (compare specification A with specification B).

The sign on collateral is not what we would have expected. This is attributable to two causes; selection bias and the simultaneity of the interest rate margin and collateral requirements in the contracting process.

5. Conclusion

The model presented here suggests that the determinants of loan decisions should be identifiable for firms that are relatively "low risk". Among riskier firms rejection decisions will be both more frequent and less systematic (with respect to identifiable firm characteristics).

For any given level of default risk, there exist a number of loan term packages which are acceptable to the lender. The potential borrower comes to the bank with a specific "offer" in mind. Applicants pay an "application fee" to have their application considered. The loan application is reviewed and either approved based on information in the application and the file [this is why age of firm works well as a predictor], or it is subjected to further evaluation.

The newer the firm, the more likely it will be subjected to a more detailed evaluation. The bank determines an acceptable set of loan terms [that produce acceptable default risks] and offers the firm a loan package. In many instances, this offer will be a refusal, as the set of loan terms that produce acceptable risk is equivalent to immediate repayment.

When sales were uncertain as in the 1980-82 period, banks offer sets contained more onerous collateral requirements in an attempt to assure loan recovery in the event that sales were deficient. In the middle of the expansion, collateral requirements were reduced and maturity restrictions eased, shifting dependence of the loan offer set from collateral to projected cash flow. Interestingly, as the recovery progressed, there was increased dissatisfaction with interest rates offered even though nominal rates were falling. The number of rejections also declined as fewer firms failed and the number of firms with longevity [a business history] increased.

TABLE 3. Regression Estimates of Interest Rate Margin
(Standard Errors in Parentheses)

	Model A	Model B
Intercept	1.7574	4.2144
	(0.1900)**	(1.4144)**
Heckman's Lambda	N.A.	-2.8258
		(1.6110)+
Prime Plus (1=yes)	-0.4096	-0.3717
	(0.1622)**	(0.1634)**
Large bank	-0.2606	-0.4494
	(0.1771)**	(0.2071)**
Medium bank	0.0019	0.0235
	(0.1895)	(0.1897)
Business age	-0.0087	-0.0038
	(0.0010)**	(0.0055)**
Debt/Equity	0.7997	0.6476
	(0.3324)**	(0.3431)
No. of Employees	-0.0013	-0.0013
	(0.0010)	(0.0010)
Collateral Posted (1=yes)	0.2807	0.2758
	(0.1585)	(0.1585)+
Maturity of Loan (months)	-0.0004	-0.0004
	(0.0004)	(0.0004)
Adjusted R Square	0.03	0.033
Sample Size	746	746

** significant at 1%
* significant at 5%
+ significant at 10%

Endnotes

1. In a sense accepting an application is a purchase of information. However, since the bank is in the business of lending money this is a fixed cost which it would pay in any case.

2. In practice, lending institutions do receive numerous applications which might be generously termed frivolous and among which they do not try to discriminate.

3. Evidence we have on the reported probability of default for "your firm" and "firms like yours" suggest that the borrower is indeed highly myopic, assessing failure probabilities to competitors that are far higher than those assigned to himself. Overall, the mean estimated probability of failure looks like it is lower than the actual failure, and dramatically under-estimates the probability of failure for his particular firm. The owner has better and more information than the bank, but assesses it very differently.

4. From the bank's perspective all features of the contract are determined by the market place. But the fees are taken as a given by the applicant. In a sense the fees are the price of admission to the negotiating session.

5. The response rate was 35%; producing a sample of 1714 cases. About 37% of the respondents reported gross annual sales of less than $350,000, 25% had a debt to assets ratio of under .20, and 50% of them borrowed one or more times per year. Only 10% of the respondents had been in business two years ar less. The survey participants classify themselves into any one of nine industry categories. The most highly represented is retailing (32%), followed by construction (14%), manufacturing (11%), and services (12%). The remaining 31% is distributed evenly over transportation, wholesale trade, agriculture, financial and professional services.

6. Attention is directed to Table 1, which is a cross section of time series. In this context we have compared respondents assessments of their loan contracts with observed real interest rates.

Appendix: Heckman's Selectivity Model

Assume that

$$y(t) = b'x(t) + e(t), \text{ and}$$
$$z^*(t) = a'w(t) + u(t) \qquad z(t) = \text{sign}(z^*(t))$$

Observations on $y(t)$ and $x(t)$ are available only when $z(t)=1$.

The two stage method is that of Heckman(1976). First a probit model relating the probability that $z(t)=1$ to a set of independent variables is estimated. Then, the probability function is used to form Heckman's lambda which is the inverse of the Mill's ratio. Lambda is then added to the first equation as an additional variable.

References

Baltensperger, E. (1978) 'Credit Rationing: Issues and Questions', Journal of Money, Credit, and Banking 10, 120-183.

Baltensperger, e. and Devinney, T. (1985) 'Credit Rationing Theory: A Survey and Synthesis', Journal of Institutional and Theoretical Economics 141, 475-502.

Blejer, M.I. and. Hillman, L.L (1982) 'A Proposition on Short Run Departures from the law-of-One-Price', European Economic Review 17, 51-60.

Carlson, J.A. and Pescatrice, D.R. (1980) 'Persistent Price Distributions,', Journal of Economic and Business 33, 21-27.

Dunkelberg, W. and J. Scott (July 1983) 'Report on the representativeness of The NFIB Sample of Small Firms in the U.S.', prepared for the SBA, Mimeo.

Heckman, J. (1976) 'Sample Selection Bias as a Specification Error', Econometrica 47, 153 - 161.

Hodgman, D. (1960) 'Credit Risk and Credit Rationing', Quarterly Journal of Economics 74, 258-278.

Kareken, J. (1957) 'Lender's Preferences, Credit Rationing, and the Effectiveness of Monetary Policy', Review of Economics and Statistics 39, 292-302.

Melnick, A. and Plaut, S. (1986) 'Loan Commitment Contracts, Terms of Lending, and Credit Allocation', Journal of Finance 41, 425-435.

Plaut, S. (1985) 'The Theory of Collateral', Journal of Banking and Finance 9, 401-419.

Stiglitz, J. (1987) 'The Dependence of quality on Price', Journal of Economic Literature.

Scott, J. and Smity, T. (1986) ' The Effect of the Bankruptcy Reform Act of 1978 on Small Business Loan Pricing', Journal of Financial Economics, 119-140.

THE IMPACT OF FINANCIAL INSTITUTION REGULATORY CHANGE ON THE FINANCING OF SMALL BUSINESS

HARRY P. GUENTHER
Walker Cisler School of Business
Northern Michigan University
Marquette, MI 49855

ABSTRACT. This paper evaluates the impact on small firm financing of : (1) the Garn-St. Germain Act of 1982; (2) steps to reform the restrictions on commercial banks'securities activities imposed by the Glass-Steagall Act; and (3) the risk-based capital guidelines. The paper analyzes the impact of each of these initiatives in terms of the following effects: (a) the effect on the volume of funds flowing to banks and savings and loan associations; (b) the effect on the allocation of funds by these lending institutions; (c) the effect on financial institution concentration and competitive structure; and (d) the effect on regulatory attitudes, interpretations, and procedures. The analysis suggests that the Garn-St. Germain Act has benefitted small firms, the Glass-Steagall reform will have a largely neutral impact, and that risk-based capital requirements will be negative.

1. Introduction

The purposes of this paper are to evaluate: (1) the extent to which major banking legislative and regulatory initiatives since 1981 have addressed the problems of small firm financing identified in the "Studies of Small Business Finance" (hereinafter "Studies") conducted under the auspices of the Interagency Task Force on Small Business, submitted to the Congress in February 1982; and (2) the degree to which these initiatives may have had, or can be expected to have, unintended adverse impacts on small firm financing. Specifically, the paper examines the three major legislative-regulatory initiatives since the "Studies": (1) the Garn-St. Germain Act of 1982; (2) efforts to revise the restrictions on commercial banks' securities activities imposed by the Glass-Steagall Act [1]; and (3) the newly promulgated risk-based capital guidelines. Such a study is important not only because the financial health of small business is important to the U.S. economy, but also because, as the three federal bank regulatory agencies noted in their Report to the Congress summarizing the conclusions of the "Studies", "Government regulations and public policy decisions often have unintended adverse impacts on small business financing."

Small firm financing problems identified in the "Studies" can be grouped into four categories:

(1) relatively high cost of funds;
(2) limited availability of funds and, regarding some financial markets, limited or non-existent access;

R. Yazdipour (ed.), Advances in Small Business Finance, 139–156.
© 1991 *Kluwer Academic Publishers. Printed in the Netherlands.*

    (3) changing competitive structure and levels of concentration in banking which might be prejudicial to the interests of small firms; and

    (4) regulatory attitudes, interpretations and/or practices which inhibit lending to small firms.

In examining the legislative and regulatory initiatives identified above, this paper analyzes the impact of each initiative on small firm financing in terms of one or more of the following effects:

    (1) the effect on the volume of funds flowing to banks and savings and loan associations, especially small ones, the traditional or likely potential suppliers of funds to small firms;

    (2) the effect on the allocation of funds by these lending institutions;

    (3) the effect on financial institution concentration and competitive structure; and

    (4) the effect on regulatory attitudes, interpretations, and procedures, especially those relating to the impact of diversification on risk.

The criteria of evaluation are simple and straightforward. Those features of the initiatives that increase the flows of funds into deposit institutions, or serve to reduce outflows, are interpreted as favorable to small firms. Those that expand the number of firms that can supply capital to small firms or create new or improved access to various financial markets likewise are viewed as favorable to small firms. Those that increase concentration among deposit institutions are considered to have a negative influence on small firm financing, but that negative influence can be offset to the extent that it enhances opportunities for asset diversification and that regulatory practices and attitudes do not interfere with recognition of the risk reducing benefits of diversification. Finally, those features that involve regulatory influences which raise the costs of extending credit to small firms, or that raise the perceived risk, or that interfere with cost or risk reduction are viewed as harmful to small firm financing. Small firms are considered to be sole proprietorships and firms with fewer than 100 employees.

Of necessity, much of the analysis and most of the conclusions are speculative. While the Garn-St. Germain Act became law long enough ago to provide a review of ex post data, the other initiatives are very recent. Glass-Steagall reform is essentially limited to the Board of Governors' ruling on applications to underwrite corporate debt and equity dated January 18, 1989. The risk-based capital guidelines were issued by the Federal Reserve in their final form on January 19, 1989, and do not become fully effective until 1992.

1.1 THE GARN-ST. GERMAIN ACT OF 1982

The significance of the Garn-St. Germain Act for small firm financing stems from its impact in three areas: (1) depository institutions' sources of funds; (2) depository institutions powers or uses of funds; and (3) financial institution competitive structure. Each area of impact is examined below.

1.1.1 Sources Of Funds. Banks, especially small banks, are extremely important sources of funds for small firms. With the expansion of S&L powers under DIDMCA and, further, under the Garn-St. Germain Act (the latter powers discussed below), S&Ls also became potentially significant sources of funds to small firms. In the late 1970s and early 1980s all deposit institutions, especially small ones which could not compete in the money markets with their own negotiable certificates of deposit, faced serious funding problems, primarily due to competition from money market mutual funds (MMMFs). Any steps that could be taken to

TABLE 1. Financial Asset and Liability Data, Selected Financial Institutions
Year-End 1977-87

(Billions of $)

	Total Financial Assets of Money Market Mutual Funds	Small Time & Savings Deposits Commercial Banks	S&Ls
1977	$ 3.9	$386.1	$377.3
1978	10.8	399.3	415.9
1979	45.2	428.8	440.7
1980	76.4	473.6	471.0
1981	186.2	513.7	474.9
1982	219.8	611.4	508.0
1983	179.4	742.2	573.7
1984	233.6	816.8	640.0
1985	243.8	897.2	685.0
1986	292.1	968.7	717.1
1987	316.1	996.1	765.7

SOURCE: Board of Governors of the Federal Reserve System, "Flow of Funds Accounts, Financial Assets and Liabilities Year-End, 1964-87" (Washington, D.C.).

enhance their ability to compete for funds would have beneficial ramifications for small firms. The Garn- St. Germain Act contained four such provisions:

(1) directions to the Depository Institutions Deregulation Committee (DIDC) to authorize an account for deposit institutions equivalent to money market mutual funds, an account which later became known as the money market deposit account;
(2) expansion of deposit institutions' NOW account powers so that the accounts could be offered to federal, state, and local governments;
(3) permission to S&Ls to offer demand deposit accounts to commercial loan customers;
(4) exemption of the first $2 million of liabilities requiring reserves from reserve require ments, with the exempted amount rising over time as bank liabilities grew.

The impact of these powers on deposit institutuion funding was both immediate and significant as shown in Table 1. While there are no available data relating these funding benefits to small firm financing, it is clear that small firms' principal existing and potential sources of non-trade credit were the recipients of major funds inflows.

1.1.2. *New Powers; Uses Of Funds.* Small firms are heavily dependent on local sources of funds which limits the competition in meeting their credit needs and reduces the number of independent sources of judgment regarding small firms' credit- worthiness. These factors, in turn, result in reduced credit availability and/or higher costs than could be expected under more competitive conditions. The Garn-St. Germain Act included several provisions which related to uses of funds by depository institutions and which were relevant to small firm financing:

 (1) effective January 1, 1984, federal S&Ls and savings banks were authorized to engage in commercial lending up to 10 percent of assets;

 (2) federal S&Ls were authorized to extend commercial real estate loans up to 40 percent of assets;

 (3) federal S&Ls were permitted to make consumer loans up to 30 percent of assets, a category defined to include inventory and floor plan financing for dealers in consumer goods; and

 (4) federal S&Ls were permitted to hold up to 10 percent of assets in personal property leasing activities.

Although the Congressional goal was increased asset diversification for thrift institutions, small firms seem likely to be major beneficiaries. Each of the expanded powers relates to commercial activities and, as shown in Table 2, commercial lending by S&Ls has increased.

TABLE 2. Selected Assets, Savings & Loan Associations Year-End, 1977-87
(Billions of $)

	Non-Mortgage Loans to Business	Open Market Paper
1977	-	$ 2.3
1978	-	2.7
1979	-	3.4
1980	-	4.9
1981	$ 0.4	6.1
1982	0.7	8.8
1983	3.1	12.5
1984	11.8	14.9
1985	17.4	19.1
1986	24.0	26.0
1987	23.8	23.4

SOURCE: Board of Governors of the Federal Reserve System, "Flow of Funds Accounts, Financial Assets and Liabilities Year-End, 1964-87" (Washington, D.C.).

The vast majority of thrift institutions are small with a local market. The effect of the provisions is to increase the number of competitors able to offer credit services to small firms. In defining consumer loans to include inventory and floor plan financing for dealers in consumer goods, the Act embraced a category of borrower which is overwhelmingly made up of small firms. And, by including leasing activities, they allowed S&Ls to enter a field expected to be of growing importance to small firms.[2]

There were two other provisions of the Act relating to uses of funds by commercial banks, the impact of which on small firms is probably mixed. On the one hand, the limitations on loans to insiders were eased, a step which is of particular importance to small banks in local markets where local entrepreneurs are likely to be among the directors of the bank and where credit alternatives may be limited. On the other hand, the loan limit to a single borrower for national banks was increased, a step which may result in some increased allocation of funds in the form of larger loans to large firms which otherwise would have been allocated to other firms including small firms.

1.1.3. Impact On Competitive Structure And Concentration. Beyond the increased competition in sources and uses of funds discussed above, there are some other aspects of the Act with relevance to structure, though their influence is mixed or uncertain. These include the acceleration of deposit interest rate deregulation, the emergency provisions for merger and acquisition of failing institutions, and the powers that facilitated regulatory forbearance.

    1. Acceleration of deposit interest deregulation.

    Deregulation can be viewed as having raised the cost of funds, thereby placing an additional premium on whatever economies of scale exist and, in turn, leading to greater concentration. However, in the absence of MMDAs, it would have been increasingly difficult for those banks and thrifts without access to the negotiable CD market to compete for funds and the stimulus to concentration well may have been even greater. Thus, on balance, the result has probably been less concentration than otherwise would have resulted.

    2. Emergency merger and acquisition powers.

    These provisions of the Act opened the door a crack to interstate banking and, perhaps, acted as a spur to subsequent state action which has led us to the verge of nationwide banking. To some degree the provisions of the Act would be both negative (by shifting sources of decision making away from the local bank) and positive (permitting better geographic diversification), thus reducing the risk profile of the combined loan portfolios. However, to the extent we measure the impact by the priorities established under the Act, the favorable and negative influences are the reverse.

The priorities for approving an acquiring institution were set as follows:

    (a) like institution, within the state;
    (b) like institution, outside the state;
    (c) unlike institution, within the state;
    (d) unlike institution, outside the state;
    (e) in considering out of state bidding, preference is given to adjacent states.

Based on these priorities it would seem likely that small firms benefitted due to the reduced likelihood that the location of decision making was shifted to another state. At the same time, the priorities served to inhibit the most positive potential acquisition in terms of geographic diversification of asset risk and accompanying potential for risk reduction.

    3. Facilitation of regulatory forbearance.

    By authorizing the issuance of net worth certificates by the insurance agencies, the

Act kept the number of competing institutions higher than otherwise would have been the case. However, subsequent history amply has demonstrated that the impact of this has been to raise the cost of funds to other, healthy institutions, thus contributing to a higher cost of funds to borrowers from those institutions. While this may have forced some institutions to gravitate to the highest available returns, including some small firm loans that otherwise would not have been made, the longer term effect has been the erosion of the risk bearing capacity of those institutions and their competitors, condemnation in some quarters of the broader powers granted to thrifts, many of which powers benefit small firms, and, perhaps, some added skepticism regarding the prudence of lending to small firms.

1.1.4 *Summary*. The results of the preceding analysis and discussion are summarized below in Exhibit 1.

EXHIBIT 1. IMPACT OF GARN-ST. GERMAIN ACT ON SMALL FIRMS

	Influence on:			
Provision:	Funds Availability	Funds Allocation	Concentration	Regulatory Attitudes
Broader Powers	Positive	Positive	Positive	None
Eased Loan Limits	None*	Neutral**	None	None
Rate Deregulation	Positive	None	Positive	None
Merger Authority	None	None	Neutral	None
Regulatory Forbearance	Negative	None	Negative	Negative

  * None : no influence identified
 ** Neutral : offsetting positive and negative influences

1.2 GLASS-STEAGALL REFORM

1.2.1. *Introduction*. Despite the extensive debate in the Congress and the overwhelming support for extensive amendment to the Glass-Steagall Act in the Senate, the law was not amended in 1988. Nevertheless, substantial marketplace change is occurring as a result of regulations issued by the bank regulatory agencies. This paper focuses on an order issued on January 18, 1989 by the Board of Governors of the Federal Reserve System[3] and, to a lesser extent, the regulation issued by the FDIC on November 19, 1984.[4] As noted earlier (footnote #1), it is these developments to which the paper refers by use of the expression Glass-Steagall "reform".

Because the law has not been amended, there are some facets of the reform which at best are awkward and, at worst, detrimental to small firms. This is inherent in a process that had to seek ways to broaden banking institutions' securities activities within the Glass-Steagall Act's restraints. Nevertheless, these shortcomings will be noted along with other features of the "reform" which seem likely to affect small firm financing.

These regulations will be analyzed in terms of their probable impact on the cost and availability of capital for small firms. The analysis considers the new powers authorized for banks by the orders or regulations and their impact on: (1) the availability of funds; (2) funds allocation; and (3) competitive structure of the banking industry.

1.2.2. *New Powers And Small Business.* The Board of Governors has authorized, subject to various conditions, certain applicant bank holding companies, through wholly-owned securities affiliates, to underwrite and deal in debt and equity securities.[5] Earlier the FDIC authorized subsidiaries of insured non-member banks to underwrite investment quality debt securities and investment quality equity securities.[6] This regulation was upheld by the D. C. Circuit Court in 1987.[7]

These new powers should have the effect of increasing competition in the market for underwriting securities[8] which, in turn, should lower the spreads and, thus, the cost to issuing firms. As these spreads narrow, so will the profits to underwriting firms. A logical by-product of shrinking profit margins would be for underwriting firms to gradually move "down- scale" to provide underwriting services to "middle market" firms,[9] just as commercial banks' lending efforts earlier shifted "down-scale" in response to large borrower firms deserting the commercial loan market in favor of commercial paper.

This process, as important as it may be in increasing the efficiency of financial markets, does not seem likely to extend far enough to directly benefit small firms. The initial benefits will be to those firms needing it least, that is, large firms. Subsequently, middle market firms will benefit. However, because of the substantial economies of scale involved in public securities offerings, it does not seem likely that the movement "down-scale" will extend to small firms.

It is important to examine not only the powers granted, but the limitations on those powers or the conditions under which they can be exercised. Several of these make it unlikely that small banking institutions will avail themselves of the powers granted or that the powers will be used to underwrite or deal in the securities of small firms. Perhaps most fundamental is the condition that underwriting be conducted by a separate securities subsidiary of a bank holding company, in the case of the Board's Order, or by a separate securities affiliate of an insured non- member bank in the case of the FDIC regulation. While in each case some such separation of the underwriting activity from the bank is necessary in order to avoid violating the restraints of the Glass-Steagall Act, it does impose a more expensive organizational framework on the activity than if conducted within the bank and thus reduces the likelihood that small banks may undertake such activities; yet, such banks could be especially helpful to small firms seeking help in developing a market for their equity capital. Unfortunately, based on the legislation that passed the Senate in 1988, it seems unlikely that, even if the Congress were to amend the Glass-Steagall Act, it would permit underwriting activity within the bank. There are two rationales for this separation: (1) safety and soundness of the bank; and (2) the avoidance of conflicts of interest. Neither rationale, however, necessitates this organizational approach. Regarding conflicts of interest, the Board considered whether to prohibit lending by a bank in connection with financing underwritten or arranged by an affiliated underwriting subsidiary and determined it was not necessary, largely on the grounds that sound management and regulatory supervision would be sufficient.[10] While implicit in this argument is the fact that the lending and underwriting are done by separate affiliates, the avoidance of conflicts of interest will result from management controls and/or supervision. As to safety and soundness, this can be effectively dealt with by imposing some quantitative limitation to exposure from securities underwritten and/or related credit extended relative to bank capital just as is done at present regarding loan limits to a single borrower.

It should be noted that the Board Order is less restrictive in this regard than the FDIC regulation covering insured non-member banks.[11] The Board's Order also is more favorable to small business than earlier ones in that it dropped the requirement that the securities underwritten or dealt in by the subsidiary be rated as investment quality.[12]

If, as seems likely and as argued above, the underwriting of and dealing in corporate securities by banking institutions will not be conducted by smaller institutions but by large ones through the framework of a bank holding company, an additional restraint on offering the service to small firms comes into play. This is the control limitation in the Bank Holding Company Act itself[13] which prohibits, without Board approval, acquisition of 5 percent or more of the voting shares of a nonbank company. Although the Board's Order states that acquisition of shares pursuant to a firm underwriting agreement would not violate the prohibitions against ownership or control even if they exceeded 25 percent of the voting shares if disposed of within 30 days and not voted,[14] there are two problems remaining. First, any effort to underwrite the shares of a small firm well may require a longer period of time for distribution than for the shares of large well-known firms. Thus, there remains an inhibition to underwriting the shares of small firms if the amount exceeds 25 percent of the shares, an event much more likely in raising capital for a small firm. Second, the exception apparently does not apply to a subsidiary's dealer function[15] so that, other than the 30 day "window" for bona fide underwriting, the ownership of shares would be permissible only up to 5 percent of voting shares.

Another limitation in the Board's 1989 Order inimical to the interests of small firms is the stipulation that the gross revenues from underwriting and dealing in ineligible securities (those not authorized under the Glass-Steagall Act) "... may not exceed 5 percent of the subsidiary's total gross revenues on average over any two year period."[16] While the provision grows out of the necessity to skirt the prohibitions in Section 20 of the Glass-Steagall Act by making sure the subsidiary is not engaged principally in underwriting or dealing in ineligible securities, the net effect of the restriction is to prevent any meaningful activity in either area unless the securities subsidiary is already engaged substantially in securities activities permissible under Glass-Steagall, such as underwriting and dealing in U. S. government securities or general obligation municipals. This all but precludes use of the authority by small banking or thrift institutions.

A final limitation in the Board's 1989 order is the approval of underwriting equity securities, but deferral of the commencement of that activity for one year at which time the Board will determine whether Applicants "... have established the managerial and operational infrastructure and other policies and procedures necessary to comply ..."[17] with the Board's order. Even if the increase in underwriting competition gradually shifts the availability of the service at reasonable cost "down-scale", the small firm really will benefit only if this applies to the underwriting of equity securities, because it is access to new sources of equity capital of which these firms have greatest need. The deferral of equity underwriting can be dismissed as unimportant in terms of its duration; after all, a year is not of much importance relative to the length of time it will take the impact of increased competition to shift "down-scale". Of far more significance than the duration of the deferral are: (1) the implicit invitation to the Congress, during this interim period, to enact legislation restricting (or prohibiting) underwriting equity securities; and (2) what regulatory details the Board of Governors may eventually develop in spelling out more precisely "managerial and operational infrastructure and other policies and procedures." Given the prevailing wisdom that underwriting is risky and equities the most risky of all securities to underwrite, there is no aspect of the Board's 1989 order more likely to come under pressure for revision or circumscription than that permitting the underwriting of equity securities.

1.2.3. *Impact On Bank Resource Allocations.* The impact of new securities powers on banks' allocation of resources should benefit the small firm over the long term. The initial impact of money center and some large regional banking institutions engaging in securities activities should be a modest easing of pressures on margins in the middle market for C&I lending. That, in turn, should encourage banks to expand such lending and be able to price such loans more appropriately for the risk involved. As pricing skills improve, some banks will expand further "down-scale" in C&I lending. Subsequently, as competition intensifies in underwriting activities due to bank entry, spreads will narrow in that business and underwriters are likely to move "down-scale" as described earlier. The result of the move "down-scale" in underwriting will be a renewal of the erosion of lending margins in the middle market, driving some banks to shift further "down-scale" in their C&I lending, a shift that will benefit small firms seeking bank credit. This process, however, will be attenuated by the impact of the risk-based capital guidelines (discussed below), so that any benefits to small firms will be marginal at best.

1.2.4. *Impact On Competitive Structure.* A key ingredient in underwriting securities profitably is placing power and/or a distribution network. The Board's order, in citing Applicant's experience in establishing distribution networks in connection with securities already being underwritten and in loan syndications, might suggest that entry into underwriting thus would intensify either the movement toward interstate bank acquisitions or toward a tightening of correspondent/respondent relationships. However, the Board's order requires that securities activities be conducted through separate affiliates. Furthermore, unlike the securities traditionally underwritten by banks and their subsidiaries (government securities) and loan syndications, the new underwriting powers involve securities in which banks themselves do not invest or cannot legally invest. As a result, whatever need may exist for a geographically widespread distribution network will be filled either by existing local retail securities firms, by non-bank affiliated members of the underwriting syndicate, or by a geographic expansion of the securities subsidiary itself.

It is conceivable, in the long run, if and when competition pushes the availability of underwriting "down-scale" far enough, that geographic expansion by a holding company's deposit gathering, money management, and lending activities will be a key to generating issuer clients. However, based on the expectation that the initial focus will be on large issuers, and on the experience of investment banking firms in serving those clients without a broad geographic network of offices, competitive structure implications appear minimal for the forseeable future.

1.2.5. *Summary.* The results of the preceding analysis and discussion are summarized below in Exhibit 2.

EXHIBIT 2. IMPACT OF GLASS-STEAGALL REFORM
Influence of New Powers on:

Funds Availability	Funds Allocation	Concentration	Regulatory Attitudes
Neutral**	Positive	Neutral	None*

   *   None   : no influence identified
 ** Neutral : offsetting positive and negative influences

1.3. RISK-BASED CAPITAL REQUIREMENTS

The impact of risk-based capital requirements on small firm financing will be felt primarily through their influence on the way in which banks allocate resources at their disposal. In addition, over a longer period of time, impact may stem from influences on competitive structure.

1.3.1. *Allocational Influence.* There are three reasons why risk-based capital requirements may have an effect on small firm financing. These can be identified as: (1) the capital adequacy effect; (2) the risk category effect; and (3) the regulatory effect. Each is discussed below.
  1. The capital adequacy effect.
   The shift to risk-base capital requirements will alter the individual bank's degree of capital adequency. For example, some formerly adequately capitalized banks will have inadequate capital or the degree of their excess capitalization[18] will be reduced. These will be referred to below as capital losers. Conversely, some banks which, prior to the new requirements, had adequate capital or excess capital will now find that they have excess or greater excess capital, respectively. These will be referred to below as capital gainers.

For those banks that are capital losers there are various possible responses. If they wish to restore their previous relative capital position, they can either increase their capital or they can reallocate resources to categories of assets which require less capital backing. For purposes of this paper it is the last group that is of concern. Any reallocation of assets from a higher risk weighted category to a lower one will offset, to some degree, the "loss" of capital adequacy. This could have a neutral impact on small firms (e.g., a shift out of a Category Three:50 percent weighted asset such as a residential mortgage into a Category One:0 percent weighted asset such as a Treasury bill. Alternatively, it might be a shift out of a Category Four:100 percent asset into some lower risk category. Because commercial and industrial loans, including loans to small firms, all are in the highest risk weighting category (Category Four:100 percent), this type of inter-category shifting to offset capital adequacy "losses" to some degree inevitably will reduce the availability of small firm financing. The only exception to this would be a bank which undertook inter-category shifts from a non-small business loan in the 100 percent risk weighted category to a 1 to 4 family first mortgage loan (50 percent risk weighted category) which was used for the homeowner's small business enterprise.

Another result of the capital adequacy effect on capital losers will be the increased incentive for loan sales and securitization, an effect regarding which there already appears to be some marketplace evidence. As these "loan sellers" are likely to continue to be primarily large banks and most of the loans sold likely to be other than C&I loans, the direct impact on small firm financing is likely to be nil for the foreseeable future. However, to the extent that increased efforts to sell loans and securitization packages makes smaller banks increasingly aware of the opportunity to buy such assets or makes their promised yields more attractive, there is a growing risk that acquisition of assets by this means will substitute for direct lending by small banks, and small firm financing will suffer.

For capital gainers the move to risk based capital presents asset reallocation opportunities which involve shifting from lower to higher risk weighting categories. While this would include making more private sector loans, including loans to small firms, there are various reasons to be skeptical that this will happen. First, most of the banks in this group are those which already have "excess" capital. Management is apparently satisfied with its existing level of risk in terms of capital. While the shift to risk-based capital measurements produces an increase in the extent to which existing capital exceeds regulatory minima, it does not alter either the absolute amount of capital or the bank's asset and liability mixes with which management presumably already was satisfied. There are two types of banks in this group: (1) those which maintain excess capital because managers "sleep better"; and (2) those with excess capital because management did not believe there were additional lending opportunities which offered adequate compensation for the risk involved. The first group is unlikely to reallocate assets because of what amounts to a change in the definition of capital. The second group consists of those banks that may have sought to gain maximum leverage of capital, but because of risk aversion allocated large portions of funds to what are now low risk weighted categories and find that under the new rules they have "excess" capital. The latter group will add assets, but there is no reason to believe they will make inter-category reallocations to higher risk groups.

2. The risk category effect.

The risk category effect results from the regulators' decision to group assets into quite broad risk weighting categories. This is especially true of Group Four:100 percent risk weighted assets which, inter alia, includes all loans to private business firms including loans to small business. There is no distinction made among various degrees of risk within this category (or any of the others) such as on the basis of default risk. Therefore, given the positive relationship between degree of default risk and promised yield on a loan, there is an incentive created by the risk weight grouping to enhance returns on capital by reallocating resources within the category; e.g., from C&I loans with relatively low promised returns to C&I loans with higher promised returns. Given that loans to small firms tend to carry higher yields,[19] on average, than loans to large firms, this intra-category reallocation could benefit small firms.

The degree to which such an intra-category reallocation may take place cannot be determined, but the three conditions under which it would take place can be described. First, it will take place to the extent to which bank management perceives that under the new guidelines regulators are more willing than heretofore to ignore default risk distinctions within the C&I loan portfolio or are more willing than heretofore to accept increments of promised return as an offset to increments of perceived default risk. (This latter factor is discussed further below under the regulatory effect.) Second, it will take place to the degree that bankers can persuade regulators that the higher yields on loans to small firms do not entail correspondingly greater risks or to the extent that such loans tend to be fully or partially secured by collateral, which so often is the case with loans to small firms. Third, such intra-category reallocation could occur to the extent that a capital loser decides to raise new capital rather than shift assets to lower risk weight categories in order to support its existing asset allocation, but is determined to maintain the level of the bank's return on equity. These potential benefits to small firms depend heavily on regulatory attitudes which are discussed below under "the regulatory effect".

3. The regulatory effect.

Historically, regulators have been unwilling to accept, beyond some undefined notion of an acceptable "norm", the argument that increments of promised returns can offset increments of perceived default risk. It in part is due to this factor that credit is rationed rather than always available if the borrower is willing to pay a high enough price. To the extent that regulators' primary focus will be pre-occupied with compliance under the risk-based guidelines (that is, with measured capital), banks, especially certain capital losers as identified above or any others which have limited their default risk because of perceived, though perhaps unarticulated, regulatory restraint, will find some window of opportunity to improve returns by shifting to higher yielding loans within the 100 percent risk weighted category, including loans to small firms. Any such benefit, however, is likely to be short-lived. The risk-based capital guidelines make clear that regulators view the risk-based capital ratio as only one step in evaluating capital adequacy. Other important factors include interest rate risk, market risk, liquidity, loan quality, and overall leverage. Not only should it not be expected that these factors will be ignored in the short-run (though possibly de-emphasized), but the guidelines seem certain to be refined over time, a refinement which will include explicitly these other factors. This probably will mean some subdivision of the 100 percent category in terms not only of default risk, but also of liquidity, market risk, and interest rate risk. On all of these criteria, small business loans seem destined to gravitate toward the high risk end of the spectrum, thus eroding over time the current incentive to intra-category reallocation. Indeed, to the extent these factors are made explicit in the process of determining capital adequacy, there is danger of increasing disincentives to lending to small firms which could leave small firm financing even less readily available than it is today.

A second, and even more disturbing regulatory effect, relates to the failure of regulators to adopt portfolio theory into their approach to evaluation of capital adequacy. The grouping of assets into broad risk categories only serves to emphasize an approach which implicitly rejects consideration of the extent to which negative correlation of returns offsets the risks of individual assets within the portfolio. Even the anticipated refinement of risk categories discussed above does not hold out promise of integration of portfolio theory. This can be especially detrimental to small firm financing because creative approaches to pooling their capital needs may hold significant potential for increasing the availability of capital and/or lowering its cost.

A final point to note is that the new capital guidelines, by permitting half the capital to be in Tier 2 capital, which is not common equity, thus making it easier to raise the required capital and/or more profitable for stockholders when the bank does so, do little for small banks. The Tier 2 category includes reserves for loan losses, preferred stock, subordinated debt, and securities that have mandatory clauses converting the issues to common stock. Except for the reserve for loan losses, small banks have little access to such sources of capital. Fortunately, the issue largely is moot because of small banks' relatively strong capital.

1.3.2. Influence On Competitive Structure. The risk-based capital guidelines are being implemented in a way that not only requires banks with "risky" asset and off-balance sheet configurations to seek more capital, but also leaves the old capital adequacy standard of 6 percent still in place even for those with low risk asset configurations. The prevailing wisdom is that the 8 percent risk-based capital adequacy figure is but an interim step on the road to a higher figure. There is far less support for the argument that the minimum level of capital adequacy for low risk banks will be lowered. As a result, the new guidelines place a substantial premium on capital and suggest that those banks with "excess" capital will continue to be attractive acquisition targets for the forseeable future. Thus the guidelines increase the incentives for further concentration in banking. As long as the market continues to exhibit a fairly strong positive correlation between risk weighted capital and a bank's price earnings ratio, those which already have relatively strong capital positions will be best situated to make additional acquisitions. Regional banking institutions tend to have stronger capital ratios and price earnings ratios than money center institutions. Because the guidelines raise minimum capital requirements and because they require that goodwill be deducted from capital thus making stock swaps the only viable method of financing an acquisition, the guidelines favor regionals over money center institutions in banking acquisitions, including interstate acquisitions. To the extent the regionals are more likely to be local C&I lenders, this will benefit small firms.

Because most of these acquisitions are initially in the form of bank holding company acquisitions (and all interstate consolidation is on that basis), the acquired institution remains a full-fledged bank rather than being merged and becoming a branch. Although this delays and/or weakens the shift in decision making away from the local level, the acquisitions serve to increase the degree of concentration of decision making and render decisions regarding asset allocation less informal, less reflective of personal knowledge of the entrepreneur's character, and less subject to local credit needs, developments likely to be detrimental to small firms. On the other hand, to the extent that the greater concentration leads to improved loan portfolio diversification, bank performance should demonstrate reduced variability which should improve the stability of credit availability. As nationwide provisions in interstate banking laws are triggered, these beneficial effects of diversification should increase. Even without appropriate regulatory response (see above), this should encourage bank management to accept risks which might have been considered excessive in the absence of the enhanced diversification opportunities stemming from further concentration.

The most significant potential structural implication of the risk-based capital guidelines is what has been referred to as the "dinosaur" thesis.[20] This argument holds that commercial banks have been all purpose or generalist financial intermediaries because of flat or non risk-based capital adequacy requirements. Under this thesis banks that might have chosen to function as pure treasury arbitrageurs (gathering deposits and investing in safe securities) were forced to make loans as well because the capital requirements were too high to yield a satisfactory return on equity from the treasury arbitrage function alone. With risk based capital adequacy, the all purpose bank will become an institution of the past (a "dinosaur") and banks will specialize, some as low risk cash management or treasury arbitrageurs, some as mortgage lenders, some as Fortune 500 lenders and underwriters, some as middle market lenders, and so on, each able to match capital to risk and so earn a return on equity satisfactory to the market. This thesis depends, of course, on the gradual regulatory willingness to consider less than 6 percent as adequate capital for very low risk (e.g., cash management arbitrageur) banks. The genesis of such speculation can be found in the guidelines themselves where the Board states that the guidelines establish a "systematic analytical framework" which, inter alia "minimizes disincentives to holding liquid, low-risk assets."[21] In terms of the focus of this paper, one question then becomes whether or not some banks will choose to specialize in loans to small business. While a handful may do so, if rich opportunities were perceived to exist in this area we would presumably see far more venture capital firms than we do. Far more likely, however, is that some banks might choose to specialize in C&I loans and, in doing so, finally get the pricing right so that it yields attractive returns, with sophisticated diversification providing a beneficial negative correlation of returns on individual loans and, thus, stability of portfolio returns. In this way banks can recapture the information advantage that made them successful at lending to large firms, an advantage they lost due to technology, pre-emptive disclosure, and mispricing.

Such specialization (i.e., in C&I lending) is likely to be undertaken only by a relatively large bank. To the extent small banks specialize they are likely to do so as cash management arbitrageurs. This will hurt small firms which have been heavily dependent upon the fact that small banks have chosen (or been forced) to be generalist institutions. Whether much larger banks in choosing to be C&I loan specialists will expand their lending down scale from the middle market sufficiently and in sufficient magnitude to offset the decline in lending to small firms by small generalist banks that become specialists in non-lending activities will determine whether the dinosaur thesis, if it is valid, serves to help or harm small firms. My guess is that it will help the largest of the small firms, those poised on the lower edge of the middle market, but that it will disadvantage the rest, especially start-up firms, at least in the short-run. In the longer term, if specialization in this area leads to better pricing, and if securitization and sale of C&I loans expands, smaller firms, too, will benefit.

1.3.3. *Summary.* The results of the preceding analysis and discussion are summarized below in Exhibit 3.

EXHIBIT 3. IMPACT OF RISK-BASED CAPITAL GUIDELINES

Impact of:	Funds Availability	Funds Allocation	Concentration	Regulatory Attitudes
Capital Adequacy Effect on:				
Capital Gainers	None*	Negative	None	None
Capital Losers	None	Neutral**	None	None
Risk Category Effect	None	Positive	None	None
Regulatory Effect	None	Negative	Neutral	Negative

> * None : no influence identivied
> ** Neutral : offsetting positive and negative influences

2. Conclusions

This paper has examined the extent to which the principal bank legislative and regulatory initiatives since 1981 have addressed the problems of small firm financing identified in the "Studies", and the degree to which these initiatives may have had, or can be expected to have, unintended adverse impacts on small firm financing. It found that while the initiatives did address some of those problems identified in the "Studies" either directly or indirectly, especially the availability and/or cost of borrowed funds, they unfortunately include a number of features that are likely to have unintended adverse impacts on small firm financing.

The overall effects of the legislative and regulatory initiatives analyzed above are shown below in Exhibit 4.

EXHIBIT 4. SUMMARY OF EFFECTS ON SMALL FIRMS

Initiative:	Funds Availability	Funds Allocation	Concentration	Regulatory Attitudes
Garn-St. Germain	Positive	Positive	Neutral**	Negative
Glass-Steagall	Neutral	Positive	Neutral	None*
Risk-Based Capital	None	Negative	Neutral	Negative

> *None: no influence identified

**Neutral: offsetting positive and negative influences

On balance, the Garn-St. Germain Act has been of benefit to small firms. Glass-Steagall reform can be expected to have a neutral to modestly positive effect, though the nature of detailed provisions removes most of the potential for benefit. The risk-based capital guidelines seem likely to have a negative impact on small firms.

Endnotes

1. This paper will refer to these efforts as "Glass-Steagall reform". However, it should be noted that attempts to amend the Glass-Steagall Act failed again in 1988 and the term "reform" refers to bank regulatory action, primarily rulings by the Board of Governors of the Federal Reserve System.

2. "High interest rates and the lack of direct access to long-term capital markets have created a major problem for the growth and well-being of small firms. Because these firms are restricted to a relatively small trade area, they also have limited access to intermediate-term funds from banks and insurance companies. The opportunity to lease needed assets has provided some relief from these financing limitations. Continued growth of the leasing industry and the aggressiveness of lessors in tailoring their services to fit the needs of individual firms will doubtless be of great benefit to the financing of small business in coming years." Bowlin, O.D. "Lease Financing: An Attractive Method of Financing Small Firms", p. 1, The Interagency Task Force on Small Business Financing (Washington, D.C. 1982).

3. Board of Governors of the Federal Reserve System, Order Conditionally Approving Applications to Engage, to a Limited Extent, in Underwriting and Dealing in Certain Securities," dated January 18, 1989; hereinafter noted as Board of Governors Order of January 18, 1989.

4. 12 CFR 337.4 (1986); these regulations were subsequently upheld by the U.S. Court of Appeals for the District of Columbia Circuit in ICI v. FDIC, No. 85-5769 (Jan. 16, 1987).

5. "(1) debt securities, including without limitation, sovereign debt securities, corporate debt, debt securities convertible into equity securities, and securities issued by a trust or other vehicle secured by or representing interests in debt obligations; and (2) equity securities, including without limitation, common stock, preferred stock, American Depositary Receipts, and other direct and indirect equity ownership interests in corporations and other entities." Board of Governors Order of January 18, 1989.

6. 12 CFR 337.4 (1986).

7. ICI v. FDIC, No. 85-5769 D.C. Cir., Jan. 16, 1987.

8. While empirical data to test this argument directly are not available, there are data available which bear on the issue indirectly. For example, the market shares of aggregate U.S. debt and equity underwriting by the top five and top ten firms during the first half of 1989 were 61 percent and 81 percent, respectively, with no commercial banking companies in the ranking; looking only at underwritings of municipal securities where commercial banks can compete, the market shares of the top five and top ten were 40 percent and 56 percent, respectively, and one commercial banking firm was among the top ten. In the non-U.S. market, where U.S. commercial banking firms also can compete, the market shares of the top five and top ten are 45 percent and 61 percent respectively and two U.S. commercial banking firms rank in the top ten. American Banker, July 5, 1989, pp. C1 and C16.

9. According to the American Banker, this is the approach many commercial banks have fol lowed in seeking to compete with investment banks in the merger advisory business. American Banker, July 3, 1989, p.11. It should not be assumed that this will benefit truly small firms. While considerable attention has been devoted to the large volume of IPOs in recent years, these have not been "small" offerings; e.g., in the first half of 1989, the average size of the 86 IPOs was $23 million. Wall Street Journal, July 17, 1989, p. C6.

10. "...sound risk management policies and procedures and the bank examination and super vision process provide an effective mechanism to control the potential for conflicts of interest and risk from lending or other participation by an affiliate bank or thrift in connection with an underwriting or similar financing transaction arranged by an underwriting subsidiary...." Board of Governors Order of January 18, 1989.

11. The FDIC regulation states that the bank shall not "(3) Extend credit or make any loan directly or indirectly to any company the stocks, bonds, debentures, notes or other securities of which are currently underwritten or distributed by such subsidiary or affiliate of the bank unless the company's stock, bonds, debentures, notes or other securities that are underwritten or distributed (i) qualify as investment quality debt securities, or (ii) qualify as investment quality equity securities...." 12 CFR 337.4 (1986).

12. Citicorp, J. P. Morgan & Co. Incorporated and Bankers Trust New York Corporation, 73 Federal Reserve Bulletin 473 (1987), aff'd. sub. nom, Securities Industry Association v. Board of Governors of the Federal Reserve System, 839 F.2d 47 (2d Cir. 1988), cert. denied, 108 S. Ct. 2830 (1988); The Chase Manhattan Corporation, 73 Federal Reserve Bulletin 607 (1987); Citicorp, 73 Federal Reserve Bulletin 618 (1987); Security Pacific Corporation, 73 Federal Reserve Bulletin 622 (1987); Chemical New York Corporation, The Chase Manhattan Corporation, Citicorp, Manufacturers Hanover Corporation, Security Pacific Cor poration, 73 Federal Reserve Bulletin 731 (1987); and J. P. Morgan & Co. Incorporated, 73 Federal Reserve Bulletin 875 (1987).

13. 12 USC section 1841.

14. Board of Governors Order of January 18, 1989, pp. 26-7, footnote 28.

15. Ibid., pp. 26-7, footnote 28.

16. Board of Governors Order of January 18, 1989, p. 3.

17. Ibid., p. 9.

18. "Excess" capitalization in the sense that capital exceeds minimum regulatory standards.

19. Bank loan data by size of borrower are not available. As a result, it is necessary to use bank size or loan size as a proxy for size of borrower. Using Federal Reserve data, both size of loan and size of bank show a negative relationship with average rate of interest charged on loans. "Terms of Lending at Commercial Banks", Federal Reserve Bulletin, Board of Governors of the Federal Reserve System, June 1989, p. A88.

156

20. Rose, Sanford, "Comment" Column, American Banker, Oct. 4, 1988, p. 1.

21. 12 CFR Part 208, Appendix A; 12 CFR Part 225, Appendix A.

Appendices

Appendix C

Appendix A

A SHORT GUIDE TO THE AVAILABLE RESEARCH IN THE FIELD OF
SMALL BUSINESS FINANCE

Rassoul Yazdipour
School of Business
California State University, Fresno
Fresno, California 93740

ABSTRACT AND INTRODUCTION Interest in conducting scholarly research in the developing field of small business finance is definitely on the rise. The best evidence for making such a claim is the drastic increase in the number of submissions of this type of work to the appropriate academic outlets over the last few years. This short paper will basically list most of the research carried out in the area of small business finance up until now.

In what follows I will list a good portion of the available literature in the area of small business finance under the following categories.

1. Small Business Access to Financial Markets
2. The Initial Public Offerings Market
3. The Venture Capital Market: Formal And Informal
4. Small Business Discontinuity and Failure
5. Ownership Effect and Company Performance
6. Others

The "Size Effect" has been extensively covered in the finance literature and therefore, there is not much need for it to be discussed in here. The reference section points to some studies in such area.

1. Small Business Access to Financial Markets

There are at least nine major studies that have dealt directly with this topic in recent years.

A. Leland and Pyle Study (1977)

B. Jensen & Meckling Study (1976)

C. Stoll Study (1984)

D. Day, Stoll, and Whaley Study (1985).

R. Yazdipour (ed.), Advances in Small Business Finance, 159–167.
© 1991 *Kluwer Academic Publishers. Printed in the Netherlands.*

E. Pettit and Singer Study (1985).

F. Fazzari, Hubbard, and Petersen Study (1988).

G. Buck, Friedman and Dunkelberge (1990)

H. Walker (1990) Study.

I. Bates Study (1990).

2. The Initial Public Offerings Market

At least six papers have directly dealt with the small business IPO.

A. Stoll and Curley Study (1970).

B. Downes and Heinkel Study (1982).

C. Ritter Study (1984).

D. Young and Zaima (1988)

E. Kryzanowski and Coallier Study (1989).

F. Krinsky and Rotenberg Study (1990).

3. The Venture Capital Market: Formal And Informal

Ten studies have specifically covered the venture capital area.

A. Huntsman and Hoban (1980).

B. Martin and Petty (1983).

C. Tyzoon and Bruno (1984).

D. Maier and Walker (1987).

E. Wetzel (1987).

F. Morgan (1988).

G. Brophy and Guthner (1988).

H. Bygrave, et al (1989).

I. Gaston (1989).

J. Yazdipour (1990).

4. Small Business Discontinuity and Failure.

There are at least three published studies in this area.

A. The Edmister Study (1972).

B. Keasey and Watson Study (1987).

C. Bates Study (1990).

5. Ownership Effects and Company Performance.

Seven studies can be listed in this section.

A. Cooley and Edwards (1982): Ownership Effects on Managerial Salaries in Small Businesses.

B. DeAnjelo and DeAnjelo (1984): Going Private: Minority Freezouts and Stockholder Wealth.

C. Trieschmann, Leverett and Shedd (1988): Valuing Common Stocks for Minority Stocks and ESOPs in Closely Held Corporations.

D. Osteryoung, Nast and Wells (1990): Pricing Minority Discounts in Closely Held Corporations.

E. Murali and Welch (1989): Agents, Owners, Control and Performance.

F. Dyl (1990): Financial Issues in Franchising.

G. Osteryoung and Wells (1989): A Valuation Model for Financial Contracts.

6. Others.

Not all the published work pertaining to the field of small business finance has been listed above. However, the accompanying reference section should provide the reader with the majority of the available studies- both published and unpublished- in this growing field.

References

Akerlof, George A. (August 1970) 'The Market for "Lemons": Quality Uncertainty and the Market Mechanism', Quarterly Journal of Economics, 488-500.

Altman, Edward I, et al (1977) 'Zeta Analysis: A New Model to Identify Bankruptcy Risk of Corporations', Journal of Banking and Finance, 1, 29-54.

Andrews, Victor L. and Peter C. Eisemann (1984) 'Who Finances Small Business in the 1980s?', in Small Business Finance: Problems in the Financing of Small Businesses, Paul M. Horvitz and R. Richardson Pettit, editors, JAI Press Inc,.

Argenti, John (1976) Corporate Collapse: The Causes and Symptoms, John Wiley and Sons.

Barry, Christopher B. and Stephan J. Brown (1984) 'Differential Information and the Small Firm Effect', Journal of Financial Economics, 13, 283-294.

Barton, Sidney L. and Paul J. Gordon (1988) 'Corporate Strategy and Capital Structure', Strategic Management Journal, Vol 9, 623-632.

Bates, Timothy, 'Financial Capital Structure and Small Business Viability', in Advances in Small Business Finance, Present volume.

Baumol, William J. (May 1968) 'Entrepreneurship in Economic Theory', American Economic Review, 65-69.

Bayless, Mark E., Susan Chaplinshy, and J. David Diltz (1988) Security Offerings And Capital Structure Theory, Working paper.

Boswell, Jonathan, 'Wy bother About Small Firms?', The Rise & Decline of Small Firms, published by George Allen Unwin Ltd.

Brock, W. A. and David S. Evans (1986) The Economics of Small Business, Holmes & Meier, N.Y.

Brophy, David J., and Mark W. Guthner, Publicly Trader Venture Capital Funds: Implications For Institutional "Fund Of Funds" Investors, Journal of Business Venturing 3, 187-206

Bruno, Albert V. and Joel K. Leidecker (Nov & Dec 1988) 'Causes of New Venture Failure: 1960s vs. 1980s', Business Horizons.

Buck, Andrew J., Joseph Friedman, William C. Dunkelberge, 'Risk and Return in Small Business Lending', in Advances in Small Business Finances, Present volum.

Bygrave, William, Norman Fast, Roubina Khoylian, Linda Vincent, and William Yue, 'Early Rates of Return of 131 Venture Capital Funds Started 1978-1984', Journal of Business Venturing 4, 93-105.

Campbell, Tim S. (Dec 1979) 'Optimal Investment Financing Decisions and the Value of Confidentiality', Journal of Financial And Quantitative Analysis, 913-924.

Constand, Richard L., Jerome S. Osteryoung, and Donald A. Nast, 'Asset-Based Financing and the Determinants of Capital Structure in the Smaller Firm: An Empirical Analysis', in Advances in Small Business Finance, Present volum.

Constand, Richard L., Jerome s. Osteryoung, and Donald a. Nast, 'Asset-Based Lending Contracts and the Resolution of Debt-Related Agency Problems' Working paper, University of Hawaii at Manoa.

Cooley, Philip L. and Charles E. Edwards (1982) 'Ownership Effects on Managerial Salaries in Small Business', Unpublished work, Trinity University.

Curley, A. and H.R. Stoll (1968) 'The Small Business Equity Gap: An Empirical Study', SBA, Washington, D.C.

Day, Theodore E., Hans R. Stoll and Robert E. Whaley (1985) Taxes, Financial Policy and Small Business. Lexington Books.

Dowens, D.H. and R. Heinkel (March 1982) 'Signalling and The Valuation of Unseasoned New Issues', Journal of Finance, 1-10.

Dwyer, Hubert J and Richard Lynn (Aug 1989) 'Small Capitalization Companies: What Does Financial Analysis Tell Us about Them?', The Financial Review, 397-415.

DeAngelo, Harry and Linda DeAngelo (Oct 1984) 'Going Private: Minority Freezouts and Stockholder Wealth', Journal of Law and Economics, 367-401.

Dyl, Edward A., 'Financial Issues In Franchising', in Advances is Small Business Finance, Present volum.

Easterwood, John C. and Ronald F. Singer, 'Are The Motivations For Leveraged Buyouts The Same For Large And Small firms?', in Advances in Small Business Finance, Present volum.

Edmister, Robert O. (March 1972) 'An Empirical Test of Financial Ratio Analysis For Small Business Failure Prediction', Journal of Financial and Quantitative Analysis, 1477-1497.

Fazzari, Steven M. and Michael J. Athey (Aug 1987) 'Asymmetric Information, Financing Constraints and Investments', The Review of Economics and Statistics, 481-487.

Fazzari, S.R., G. Hubbard, and B.C. Petersen (1987) 'Financial Constraints and Coprate Investment', National Bureau of Economic Research, Working paper, N0 2387, Cambridge, MA.

Feldstein, Martin and Jerry Green (Mar 1983) 'Why Do Companies Pay Dividends?', American Economic Review, 17-30.

Fells, George (Spring 1989) 'Venture Capital: Coping with Growth', Business Quarterly.

Friend, Irwin and Joel Hasbrouck (1988) 'Determinants of Capital Structure' in Research in Finance, Andrew H. Chen, editor, Volume 7, JAI Press Publisher.

Gaston, R.J. (1989) 'The Scale of Informal Capital Markets', Small Business Economics: An International Journal, vol 1, No, 3, 223-231.

Guenther, Harry P. The Impact of Financial Institution Regulatory Change on the Financing of Small Business', in Advances in Small Business Finance, Present volum.

Haugen, Robert A. and Lemma W. Senbet (Mar 1988) 'Bankruptcy and Agency Costs: Their Significance to the Theory of Optimal Capital Structure', Journal of Financial and Quantitative Analysis, 27-38.

_____, (June 1981) 'Resolving the Agency Problem of External Capital Through Options', Jounal of Finance, 629-647.

Huntsman, Blaine and James P. Hoban, Jr. (Summer 1980) 'Investment in New Enterprise: Some Empirical Observations on Risk, Return, and Market Structure', Financial Management.

Horvitz, Paul M. (1984) 'Problems in the Financing of Small Business: Introduction and summary', in Small Business Finance: Problems in Financing Small Businesses, 1984, Paul M. Horvitz and R. Richardson Pettit, editor, JAI Press Publisher.

Jensen, M. C., and W. H. Meckling (1976) 'Theory of The Firm: Managerial Behavior, Agency Costs and Owership Structure', Journal of Financial Economics, Vol 11, 5-50.

Keasey, K. and R. Watson (Autumn 1987) 'Non-Financial Symptoms and the Prediction of Small Company Failure: A Test of Argenti's Hypotheses', Journal of Business Finance & Accounting, 14(3).

Krinsky, I. and W. Rotenberg (June 1989) 'Signalling and the Valuation of Unseasoned New Issues Revisited', Journal of Financial and Quantitative Analysis, Vol. 24, No.2.

Krinsky, I. and W. Rotenberg (1991) 'The Valuation of Initial Public Offerings: The Small Firm Case', in Advances in Small Business Finance, Present volum.

Kryzanowski, Lawrence and Robert Coallier (1989) 'The Motivations and Experiences of IPO Issuers of QSSP-Eligible Equities', Paper presented at The First Annual Small Firm Financial Research Sysposium.

Lane, William R. (April 1988) 'Founders, Ownership Structure and Financial Performance' Working paper, Louisiana State University.

Lease, Ronald C., John J. McConnell, and Wayne H. Mikkelson (1987) 'The Evidence on Limited Voting Stock: Motives and Consequences', Midland Coporate Finance, 66-71. Journal.

Leland, H. E., and D. H. Pyle (May 1977) 'Information Asymmetries, Financial Structure and Financial Intermediation', Journal of Finance, 371-387.

MacMillan, Ian C. and David M. Kulow (1988) 'Venture Capitalists' Involvement in Their Investment: Extent and Performance', Journal of Business Venturing 4, 27-24.

McConnell, John J. and R. Richardson Pettit (1984) 'Application of the Modern Theory of Finance to Small Business Firms', in Small Business Finance: Problems in Financing Small Businesses, Paul M. Horvitz and R. Richardson Pettit, editors, JAI Press Publisher.

Maier, John B. and David A. Walker (1987) 'The Role of Venture Capital In Financing Small Business', Journal of Business Venturing 2, 207-214 .

Martin, John D. and J. William Petty (Sept 1983) 'An Analysis of the Performance of Publicly Traded Venture Capital Companies', Journal of Financial and Quantitative Analysis, Vol. 18, No.3.

Miller, Alex, Bob Wilson, and Mel Adams, 'Financial Performance Patterns of New Corporate Ventures: An Alternative To Traditional Measures', Journal of Business Venturing 3, 287-300.

Miller, Danny (Nov 1977) 'Common Syndromes of Business Failures', Business Horizons, 43-53.

Miller, Edward M., 'A Comparison of Large And Small Firm Productivity, Labor Compensation, And Investment Rates', Review of Business & Economic Research.

Morgan, Alfred D. (1988) 'The Public Shell: Vehicle For Venture Financing', Journal of Business Venturing 3, 59-76.

Myers, Stewart C. (July 1984) 'The Capital Structure Puzzle', The Journal of Finance, 575-591.

Myers, S. C. and N. S. Majluf (June 1984) 'Corporate Financing and Investment Decisions when Firms Have Information that Investors Do Not Have', 1984, Journal of Financial Economics, 187-222.

Murali, R. and J. B. Welch (Summer 1989) 'Agents, Owners, Control and Performance', Journal of Business Finance & Accounting, 385-398.

Osteryoung, Jerome S., Donald A. Nast and William H. Wells, 'Pricing Minority Discounts in Closely-Held Corporations', in Advances in Small Business Finance, Present volum.

Osteryoung, Jerome S. and William H. Wells, 'A Valuation Model for Financial Contracts', 1989, Working Paper, Florida State University, Tallahassee.

Ou, Charles, 'Financing New Businesses', Paper presented at the 1989 Annual Meeting of The Financial Management Association.

Pettit, R. Richardson and Ronald F. Singer (Autumn 1985) 'Small Business Finance: A Research Agenda', Financial Management, 47-60.

Prasad, Dev (1989) 'Conveying Project Quality Through Signals: An Empirical Study of Initial Public Offerings', paper presented at the First Annual Small Firm Financial Research Symposium.

Ragazzi, Giorgio (1981) 'On The Relation Between Ownership Dispersion And The Firms's Market Value', Journal of Banking and Finance 5.

Ritter, Jay R. (1987) 'The Costs of Going Public', Journal of Financial Economics 19, 269-281.

Rosen, Corey (Jan/Feb 1989) 'The Growing Appeal of the Leveraged ESOP', The Journal of Business Strategy.

Ross, Stephen A. (Spring 1977) 'The Determination of Financial Structure: The Incentive Signalling Approach', The Bell Journal of Economics, 23-40.

Sahlman, William A. (Summer 1988) 'Aspects of Financial Contracting in Venture Capital', Journal of Applied Corporate Finance, 23-36.

Small Business Administration (1988) The State of Small Business: A Report of the President, Small Business Administration, Washington, D.C.

_____, (1988) Small Business in the American Economy, 1988, Small Business Administration, Washington, D.C.

Siegel, Robin, Eric Siegel, and Ian C. MacMillan (1988) 'Corporate Venture Capitalists: Autonomy, Obstacles, and Performance', Journal of Business Venturing 3, 233-247.

Stoll, Hans R. (1984) 'Small Firms' Access to Public Equity Financing', in Small Business Finance: Problems of Financing Small Businesses, Paul M. Horvitz and R. Richardson Pettit, editors, JAI Press Publisher.

Stoll, Hans R. and Anthony J. Curley (Sept 1970) 'Small Business And The New Issues Market For Equities', Journal of Financial and Quantitative Analysis, 309-322.

Stonehill, Arthur, et al (Autum 1975) 'Financial Goals And Debt Ratio Determinants: A Survey of Practice In Five Countries', Financial Management, 27-41.

Trieschmann, James S., E.J. Leverett, and Peter J. Shedd (March-April 1988) 'Valuating Common Stock For Minority Stock and ESOPs in Closely Held Corporations', Business Horizons.

Tyzoon, Tyebjee T. and Albert V. Bruno (Sept 1984) 'A Model of Venture Capitalist Investment Activity', Management Science Vol. 30, No. 9.

Tzang, Dah-nein (May 1989) 'Risk Sharing In Participation Loan Arrangements: An Agency Problem Approach', Working papers.

Walker, David A. (1991) 'An Empirical Analysis of Financing the Small firm', in Advances in Small Business Finance, Present volum.

Walker, David A. (1989) 'Financing the Small firm', Small Business Economics: An International Journal, vol1, No 4, 285-296.

Walker, David A. (Winter 1985) 'Trade Credit Supply for Small Businesses', American Journal of Small Business, IX(3), 30-40.

Walker, E.W., and J. William Petty (Winter 1978) 'Financial Differences Between Large and Small Firms', Financial Management, 61-68.

Warner, Jerold B. (May 1977) 'Bankruptcy Costs: Some Evidence', The Journal of Finance, 337-347.

Wolfe, Glenn A. and Elizabeth s. Cooperman (Oct 1987) 'A Reassessment of the "Excess Return Phenomenon" for Initial Public Offerings of Common Stock', Paper presented at the Financial Management Association.

Wetzel, William E. Jr. (1987) 'The Informal Venture Capital Market: Aspects of Scale and Market Efficiency', Journal of Business Venturing 2, 299-313.

Yazdipour, Rassoul (1990) 'An Empirical Analysis of the Market for Formal Venture Capital', Small Business Economics: An International Journal, 2, 33-39.

Yazdipour, Rassoul, (1989) 'The State of Research in The Field of Small Business Finance', California State University-Fresno, Working paper.

Yazdipour, Rassoul, and Moon H. Song (1990) 'Toward A Theory of Optimum Contracting in the Agent-Principal Relationship', California State University-Fresno, Working paper.

Young, John E., and Janis K. Zaima (1988) 'The Aftermarket Performance of Small Firm Initial Public Offerings', Journal of Business Venturing, 77-87.

Appendix B

AVAILABLE FINANCIAL DATA BASES FOR RESEARCH ON SMALL BUSINESS

CHARLES OU, Ph.D.
Office of Economic Research
Small Business Administration
Washington, D.C. 20416

1. Introduction

Lack of statistical information has plagued small business finance researchers in the past. There has been no systematic effort to collect the information on a regular basis. Increasing interests in small business financial issues has resulted in collection of data by institutions and individual researchers. Most of these efforts are special purpose surveys conducted to collect data for a specific issue under investigation.

The purpose of this paper is to survey these existing data sources in the U.S.. In order to be selected, a data source had to meet one of the two criteria : (1) data were collected and made available on a regular basis and (2) data were for general purpose and for a "general" representative population of small business. Each source will be discussed in a standard format describing the source, the publication(s), data elements, reporting frequency, reporting lag, size and SIC classification, and comments. Several important but specific surveys conducted as part of a special study either to answer very specific questions or for a special group of business will also be listed.

2. Available Data Bases

2.1. BOARD OF GOVERNORS OF THE FEDERAL RESERVE SYSTEM

Survey of terms of bank loans to businesses and farms

Publication(s): (1) 'Survey of Terms of Bank Lending: (Statistics Release E.2)', (Washington, D.C.: Board of Governors of the Federal Reserve System); (2) Federal Reserve Bulletin

Brief Description: Survey of approximately 300 banks of all the business loans made during the first week of the months of February, May, August and November.

Finance Related Data Elements: Interest Rates, Size of Loans, Maturity, loan participation status.

R. Yazdipour (ed.), Advances in Small Business Finance, 169–179.
© 1991 *Kluwer Academic Publishers. Printed in the Netherlands.*

Frequency of Reference: Months of February, May, August and November of the year.

Report Lag: 2 months

Size Group: For loan size groups: under 25,000, 25,000 to 49,9999, 50,000 to 99,999, 100,000 to 499,999, 500,000 to 999,999 and 1 million and over.

SIC: All commercial and industrial loans, construction and land development loans, and loans to farmers.

Comments: No information on business size.

2.2. NATIONAL FEDERATION OF INDEPENDENT BUSINESS

'Survey of Credit, Banks and Small Business'

Publication(s): (1) 'Credit, Banks and Small Business' (Washington, D.C.: NFIB Foundation, 1982); (2) 'Credit, Banks and Small Business 1980-1984' (Washington, D.C.: NFIB Foundation, 1985); (3) 'Small Business and Banks: The U.S' (Washington, D.C.: NFIB Foundation, 1988)

Brief Description: Survey of about 2,500 members of their borrowing experience from commercial banks. Emphasis of special issues in different surveys.

Finance Related Data Elements: Uses of business loans, terms of most recent loans, availability of loans, bank services, and major concerns with bank lending and credit market.

Frequency of Reference Period: Every two to three years.[1]

Reporting Lag: Varied
Size Group: Varied

SIC: Varied, but limited to one digit SIC only.

Comments: (1) For over 500,000 members of the NFIB
(2) Limited to borrowing from the banks
(3) Micro data may be obtained from the NFIB

2.3. ROBERT MORRIS ASSOCIATES

Survey of financial statements of bank borrowers.

Publication(s): RMA Annual Statement Studies (Philadelphia, PA: Robert Morris Associates)

Brief Description: Financial statements of borrowers of member banks of RMA were processed annually for the report.

Finance Related Data Elements: Major balance sheet and income statement items.

Frequency of Reference Period: Annual

Reporting Lag: 1 year

Size Group: Asset size; 2 to 4 size groups

SIC: For approximately 350 4 digits SIC industries.

Comments: (1) Not a data base for statistical analysis because the statements used in the publication "are not selected by any random or statistically reliable method".
(2) Median values for some ratios were also provided.
(3) Micro data may be available from the RMA

2.4. DUN & BRADSTREET CORPORATION, DUN & BRADSTREET CREDIT SERVICES

Survey of financial statements

Publication(s): (1) Industry Norm and Key Business Ratios Library edition and separate industry volumes.

Brief Description: Some 800,000 to 1 million financial statements are collected by Dun & Bradstreet and processed to produce financial ratios for representative firms for over 800 industries (or lines of business).

Finance Related Data Elements: Major balance sheet items, sales and profit, and key ratios.

Frequency of Reference Period: Annual

Reporting Lag: The database is updated continuously. However, publications lag 6-9 months.

Size Group: Varied

Comments: (1) Not a data base for statistical analysis because the statements are not collected through a statistically designed process. Some of the samples are very small, and, therefore, 'may not present true picture of an entire line of business.'
(2) Micro data available from Dun & Bradstreet

2.5. STANDARD AND POOR'S COMPUSTAT SERVICES, INC.

Survey of financial reports of publicly traded corporations

Publication(s): Public use tapes available

Brief Description: Collection of financial statements such as 10-K reports, filed with the U.S. Securities and Exchange Commission by publicly trade corporations. Some 1,500 small corporations are included in the database.

Finance Related Data Elements: Detailed information contained in the financial statements

Frequency of Reference Period: Annual or quarterly

Reporting Lag: Continuously updated

Size Group: Micro data[2]

SIC: Micro data[2]

Comments: (1) Most smaller publicly traded corporations in the OTC and regional exchanges are not included.
(2) These corporations are a special group of business.

2.6. BOARD OF GOVERNORS OF THE FEDERAL RESERVE SYSTEM AND THE SMALL BUSINESS ADMINISTRATION

Survey of small businesses on their business finances(NSSBF)

Publication(s): Gregory Elliehausen, John Wolken and Brenda Cox, 'The National Survey of Small Business Finances: Description and Preliminary Evaluation', in Finance and Economic Discussion Series, No. 93, Federal Reserve Board (Washington, D.C.: 1989)

Brief Description: The NSSBF collected data from a national sample of 3,600 small business firms on their use of various financial services by source as well as obtaining a balance sheet, income statement and other characteristics of the businesses.

Finance Related Data Elements: Use of deposit services—checking, savings; use of credit—leases, lines of credit, mortgages, equipment loans, etc.; use of other financial services and trade credit; and balance sheet and income statement items.

Frequency of Reference Period: One time survey

Report Lag: A public use tape will be available in the spring of 1991.

Size Group: Varied

SIC: Varied; but limited to one digit because of sample size.

Comment: With the availability of a public use tape which will contains microfirm data, the researcher can manipulate the database at his/her discretion.

2.7. U.S. DEPARTMENT OF COMMERCE, BUREAU OF CENSUS

Survey of Business Owner Characteristics

Publication(s): <u>1982 Characteristics of Business Owners</u> (Washington, D.C.: Government Printing Office, 1987)

Brief Description: A survey of 100,000 owners of sole proprietorships and small partnerships and Subchapter S Corporations (with fewer than 10 owners) in the U.S. to collect information on their personal attributes as well as the attributes of their businesses.

Finance Related Data Elements: Owner's attributes; attributes of business startups—modes of business startup, sources and amount of startup capital; and business income and employment.

Frequency: Every five years (Years ending in 2 and 7)

Reporting Lag: Data for 1982 were collected in 1986 and made available to the public in August 1987.

Size Group: By employment and sale size

SIC: All major industries listed in the Enterprise Standard Industrial Classification (ESIC).

Comments: (1) Data for 1987 are scheduled for release in November 1991.
(2) Tabulation of micro data can be made through the Bureau of Census.

2.8. SMALL BUSINESS ADMINISTRATION

Survey of Informal Investors

Publication(s): Robert Gaston and Sharon Bell, 'The Informal Supply of Capital', A Report submitted to the U.S. Small Business Administration, Office of Advocacy, Contract No. SBA-2024-AER-87, (Washington, D.C.: 1988)

Brief Description: A survey of 435 investors (from three separate surveys conducted by Applied Economics Group and Aram Research Associates) on investors characteristics, their investment preference and investment activities.

Finance Related Data Elements: Demographic characteristics of investors, business characteristics of their investments, investment preferences, and magnitudes of their investment.

Frequency of Reference Period: One time survey.

Reporting Lag: N/A

Size Group: N/A

SIC: Varied

Comment: The surveys were conducted between 1983-1986.

2.9. INTERAGENCY TASK FORCE ON SMALL BUSINESS FINANCE

Survey of Banks' Business Lending

Publication(s): 'Survey of Commercial Bank Lending to Small Business' (in <u>Studies on Small Business Finance</u>, A Report to Congress by Interagency Task Force on Small Business Finance; Washington, D.C.:   1982)

Brief Description: Survey of a national sample of 224 general banks and 25 special banks in the U.S.

Finance Related Data Elements: Bank organization of small business lending function; credit availability; small business loan characteristics; small business loan pricing and profitability; and banks' participation in government program.

Frequency of Reference Period: One time survey

Reporting Lag: N/A

Size Group: Three bank sizes were used in tabulating the data: banks with asset under $100 million, 100 million to under $1 Billion and assets $1 billion and over.

SIC: Limited

Comment: The most comprehensive survey of bankers on their lending to small businesses. Micro data are not available to public.

2.10. BOARD OF GOVERNORS OF THE FEDERAL RESERVE SYSTEM

Survey of consumer finances of households

Publication(s): (1) 'Survey of Consumer Finance 1983', <u>Federal Reserve Bulletin</u>, September 1984; (2) 'Survey of Consumer Finance, 1983: A second report', <u>Federal Reserve Bulletin</u>, December 1984; (3) 'Financial Characteristics of High-Income Families', <u>Federal Reserve Bulletin</u> March 1986.

Brief Description: Survey of households of their household finances. A subsample of high income families allows an estimate of holdings of privately-held businesses by American households. Of 3,800 family respondents, over 400 had income over $50,000.

Finance Related Data Elements: Value of business assets by individual business, management role of the owner, debt of/to the business owner, business income, gross receipts and share of retained earnings.

Frequency of Reference Periods: Varied. A shorter version of the survey was conducted in 1987. The 1989 Survey of Consumer Finance is in progress.

Reporting Lag: Findings are made available in reports. A public use tape for 1983 survey was made available to the public in 1986.

Size Group: Varied

SIC: Varied

Comments: (1) Survey of owners, not of businesses.
(2) Limited information of business finances were asked in the 1983 survey.
(3) Two other household surveys which also ask business ownership information are (a) Bureau of Census, 'Current Population Survey' (quarterly, for self-employed owners of business) and (b) Bureau of Census, 'Survey of Income and Program Participation' (quarterly, with some asking questions on business information owned by individuals).

2.11. U.S. DEPARTMENT OF COMMERCE, BUREAU OF CENSUS

Survey of financial statements of manufacturing, mining, and trade corporations.

Publication(s): Quarterly Financial report for Manufacturing, Mining, and Trade Corporations (Government Printing Office)

Brief Description: Quarterly survey of financial statements for 7,800 manufacturing, 1,700 wholesale trade, 970 retail trade, and 500 mining corporations for information on corporate profit and other information.

Finance Related Data Elements: Major balance sheet and income statement items.

Frequency of Reference Periods: Quarterly

Reporting Lag: 6 months

Size Group: Varied. For all manufacturing corporations, there are three small size groups—asset under $5 million, $5 to $10 million and $10 to $25 million. For 2 digit manufacturing corporations, there is only one small size with assets under $25 million .

SIC: 2 digit SIC for manufacturing corporations

Comments: (1) Sample size for firms with asset under $5 million is small and many values are estimated rather than collected for this group.
(2) Data are available in aggregate values. No microfirm data is available for use by researchers.

2.12. U.S. DEPARTMENT OF TREASURY, INTERNAL REVENUE SERVICE

Sample of tax return data filed by businesses.

Publication(s): (1) <u>Corporate Source Book of Statistics of Income</u> (Washington, D.C.: Internal Revenue Service); (2) <u>SOI Bulletin</u> (Washington, D.C.: Government Printing Office)

Brief Description: Samples of annual tax returns submitted to IRS were processed by the Statistics of Income Division for financial information on U.S. corporations, partnerships, and sole proprietorships.[3]

Finance Related Data Elements: Detailed list of balance sheet and income statements items as compiled from tax returns filed with the IRS. No balance sheet data are collected for sole proprietorships.

Frequency of Reference Period: Annual

Reporting Lag: 3 years

Size Group: 12 asset size groups, including $1-$100,000, $100,000-$250,000,, $250,000-$500,000, $500,000-$1 million, $1 million-$5 million, $5 million to $10 million groups for small corporations.

SIC: About 180 two-to-three digits SIC industries.

Comments: (1) For partnerships and sole proprietorships, tabulations for industry and size are not available in the published reports.
(2) Data are available in aggregate values only.

2.13. BOARD OF GOVERNORS OF THE FEDERAL RESERVE SYSTEM

Estimates of aggregate values for the balance sheets of all major sectors in the U.S.

Publication(s): <u>Balance Sheets for the U.S. Economy</u> (Washington, D.C.: Federal Reserve Board)

Brief Description: Annual estimates of major items in the sector's balance sheet. Major sectors include households, farm, nonfarm noncorporate business, nonfarm corporate business, private financial institutions.

Finance Related Data Elements: Major balance sheet items for Nonfarm Noncorporate Business such as tangible assets and financial assets and liabilities.

Frequency of Reference Period: Annual

Reporting Lag: 1 year

Size Group: For all nonfarm noncorporate business.[4]
SIC: All nonfinancial business only.

Comment: Estimates of aggregate values for nonfarm noncorporate business are subject to large revision.

2.14. BOARD OF GOVERNORS OF THE FEDERAL RESERVE SYSTEM

Estimates of aggregate values on sources and uses of funds by major sectors in the U.S.

Publication(s):   (1) Flows of Funds Accounts (Washington, D.C.: Board of Governors of the Federal Reserve System); (2) Flow of Funds Accounts—Financial Assets and Liabilities (washinton, D.C.: Federal Reserve Board)

Brief Description: Quarterly estimates of sources and uses of funds by major sectors and by market instruments.

Finance Related Data Elements: Major sources and uses of funds such as income, capital expenditure, and changes in financial investment and liabilities.

Frequency of Reference Periods: Quarterly

Reporting Lag: 6 months

Size Group: For nonfarm noncorporate business only.[5]

SIC: All nonfarm, nonfinancial business only.

3. Some Studies Providing Other Types Of Data Sources

The following studies each conducted a survey on small business finances. Though limited in scope—in geographic or in industry coverage or in areas of issues covered, much useful information are collected by these surveys.

1. Council for Northeast Economic Action, (May 1984) An Empirical Analysis of Unmet Credit Demand in U.S. Capital Markets, (Washington, D.C., Prepared for U.S.Department of Commerce, Economic Development Agency).

2. Council for Northeast Economic Action, (June 1982) An Empirical Analysis of Unmet Credit Demand in a National Sample of the Business Population, (Washington, D.C., Prepared for Economic Development Agency, U.S. Department of Commerce).

3. Robert Combs, G. Pulver and Ron Shaffer, Financing New Small Business Enterprise in Wisconsin, Department of Agricultural Economics, University of Wisconsin.

4. Institute for Social Research, University of Michigan (1985) Measuring the Flow

of Capital and Credit to Small Firms: A Pilot Study, (Washington, D.C., Office of Advocacy, U.S. Small Business Administration).

5. JACA, (1985) 'Access to Capital by Subcategories of Small Business', A Report prepared for Small Business Administration, Office of Advocacy, Contract No. SBA-6061-OA-82, Washington, D.C.

6. Deborah Markley (1988) 'The Impact of Interstate Banking on Rural Credit Availability in the New England Region', a Project funded by the Ford Foundation. See also 'Rural and Small Business Capital Gaps: Empirical Evidence and Policy Implications'.

7. Paul Reynolds and Steven West (1985) 'New Firms in Minnesota: Their Contributions to Employment and Exports, Startup Problems and Current Status', Draft Report, Center for Urban and Regional Affairs, University of Minnesota.

8. Ron Shaffer, et. al. (1989) 'Rural Nonfarm Business Access to Debt and Equity Capital', A report submitted to U.S. Department of Agriculture and Department of Commerce, Madison, Wisconsin.

Endnotes

1. The NFIB 'Quarterly Economic Survey' included questions on "interest rate paid", "loan availability" and "expectation of financing conditions". The results are reported quarterly in Quarterly Economic Report for Business (Washington, D.C.: NFIB Foundation).

2. Researchers can mainpulate the database subjected to the limitation of the sample size.

3. Data for partnership and sole proprietorships are no longer available in detailed SIC and Size groups.

4. The balance sheet for the small nonfinancial corporate sector can not be separated from the all corporation sector.

5. The accounts for small nonfinancial corporate businesses can not be separated from all corporations.

Biographical   Sketches

Andrew Buck earned a Ph.D. in Economics form the University of Illinois at Champaign - Urbana. He is an Associate Professor of Economics at Temple University in Philadelphia.

William C. Dunkelberg earned a Ph.D. in Economics form the University of Michigan. He is the Dean of the School of Business and Management and a Professor of Economics a Temple University in Philadelphia. Dr. Dunkelberg is also the Chief Economist of the National Federation of Independent Business. Dr. Dunkelberg was a faculty member at Stanford University and Purdue University.

Edward A. Dyl is Professor of Finance and Real Estate at the University of Arizona, Tucson, Arizona. He Previously served on the faculties at the University of Wyoming, the University of San Francisco, and the University of Texas-Austin. He is past-president of the Western Finance Association and the Financial Management Association.

John C. Easterwood is an Assistant Professor of Finance at the University of Houston. His research focuses on the structure of ownership claims as a means of resolving agency and information problems, the market for corporate control, and futures markets. His publications have appeared in the Journal of Futures Markets and the California Management Review.

Joseph Friedman earned a Ph.D. in economics form the university of California at Berkeley. He is a Professor of Finance and a Chairman of the Department of Finance at Temple University in Philadelphia. Dr. Friedman also taught at Tel Aviv University and the University of Pennsylvania. Dr. Friedman held non-academic positions at the Rand Corporation in Santa Monica, California, Abt Associates in Cambridge, Massachusetts and the World Bank.

Harry P. Guenther is a professor in the Department of Accounting and Finance at the Cisler School of Business, Northern Michigan University in Marquette, Michigan. His prior positions include President of Golembe Associates, a nationally known bank research and consulting firm; Executive Vice President and Economist of the Conference of State Bank Supervisors; and Dean of the Georgetown University School of Business. He has consulted on a wide range of financial institution regulatory issues and written extensively on bank regulation, LDC debt resolution and Arab financial institutions.

Itzhak Krinsky is an Associate Professor and Chairman, Finance and Business Economics Area, in the Faculty of Business, at McMaster University, Hamilton, Ontario, Canada. Dr. Krinsky has conducted research n insurance, financial markets, investment, and econometrics. His current research interests include the development and implementation of FMS, investment decisions in manufacturing, and econometrics. He has previously published in the Journal of Financial and Quantitative Analysis, Journal of International Money and Finance, Review of Economics and Statistics, Naval Research Logistics Quarterly, Journal of Risk and Insurance, European Journal of Operational Research and many others.

Wendy Rotenberg is an Assistant Professor of Finance in the Faculty of Business at McMaster University, Hamilton, Ontario, Canada. Dr. Rotenberg's research interests include financial markets, international finance and accounting and corporate reorganization. Her previous publications have appeared in the Journal of Financial and Quantitative Analysis, Contemporary Accounting Research and the Journal of Accounting Literature, among others.

Ronald F. Singer is an Associate Professor of Finance at the University of Houston. His research interests include corporate bond valuation, option pricing, the impact of alternative bond indenture provisions on firm value, the market for corporate control, and bidding strategies in auction markets. His work has been published in journals such as Journal of Finance, Journal of Financial Economics, Journal of Business, Financial Management, and Financial Analysts Journal.

David A. Walker is Professor of Finance and Director of the Center for Business-Government Relations at the Georgetown University School of Business. He also serves as Vice President of the Financial Management Association, a national academic and practitioner association. He formerly served as the School's Associate Dean for Graduate Programs and as Executive Editor for the Journal of Financial Research. Dr. Walker is biographed in Who's Who in the East and Who's Who in Finance and Industry. He joined the Georgetown University faculty in 1980, after serving as Director of Research for the Office of the Comptroller of the Currency and Financial economist for the Federal Deposit Insurance Corporation for ten years.

Rassoul Yazdipour is an associate professor of finance at California State University, Fresno, California. He received his MBA in finance from Indiana University and his Ph.D.in Business Administration from The Ohio State University. Dr. Yazdipour is the Founding Editor of The Journal of Small Business Finance. He is also the originator of the Annual Small Firm Financial Research Symposia, now in the third year. Dr. Yazdipour has been the moderator of special sessions on small business finance at the last two annual meetings of the Financial Management Association. His research interests include international finance, venture financing, market for corporate control, and agency theory.

FINANCIAL AND MONETARY POLICY STUDIES

* 1. J.S.G. Wilson and C.F. Scheffer (eds.): *Multinational Enterprises*. Financial and Monitary Aspects. 1974   ISBN 90-286-0124-4

* 2. H. Fournier and J.E. Wadsworth (eds.): *Floating Exchange Rates*. The Lessons of Recent Experience. 1976   ISBN 90-286-0565-7

* 3. J.E. Wadsworth, J.S.G. Wilson and H. Fournier (eds.): *The Development of Financial Institutions in Europe, 1956–1976*. 1977   ISBN 90-286-0337-9

* 4. J.E. Wadsworth and F.L. de Juvigny (eds.): *New Approaches in Monetary Policy*. 1979   ISBN 90-286-0848-6

* 5. J.R. Sargent (ed.), R. Bertrand, J.S.G. Wilson and T.M. Rybczynski (ass. eds.): *Europe and the Dollar in the World-Wide Disequilibrium*. 1981 ISBN 90-286-0700-5

* 6. D.E. Fair and F.L. de Juvigny (eds.): *Bank Management in a Changing Domestic and International Environment*. The Challenges of the Eighties. 1982
                                                                    ISBN 90-247-2606-9

* 7. D.E. Fair (ed.) in cooperation with R. Bertrand: *International Lending in a Fragile World Economy*. 1983   ISBN 90-247-2809-6

  8. P. Salin (ed.): *Currency Competition and Monetary Union*. 1984
                                                                    ISBN 90-247-2817-7

* 9. D.E. Flair (ed.) in cooperation with F.L. de Juvigny: *Government Policies and the Working of Financial Systems in Industrialized Countries*. 1984 ISBN 90-247-3076-7

 10. C. Goedhart, G.A. Kessler, J. Kymmell and F. de Roos (eds.): *Jelle Zijlstra, A Central Banker's View*. Selected Speeches and Articles. 1985   ISBN 90-247-3184-4

 11. C. van Ewijk and J.J. Klant (eds.): *Monetary Conditions for Economic Recovery*. 1985
                                                                    ISBN 90-247-3219-0

* 12. D.E. Fair (ed.): *Shifting Frontiers in Financial Markets*. 1986   ISBN 90-247-3225-5

 13. E.F. Toma and M. Toma (eds.): *Central Bankers, Bureaucratic Incentives, and Monetary Policy*. 1986   ISBN 90-247-3366-9

* 14. D.E. Fair and C. de Boissieu (eds.): *International Monetary and Financial Integration*. The European Dimension. 1988   ISBN 90-247-3563-7

 15. J. Cohen: *The Flow of Funds in Theory and Practice*. A Flow-Constrained Approach to Monetary Theory and Policy. 1987   ISBN 90-247-3601-3

 16. W. Eizenga, E.F. Limburg and J.J. Polak (eds.): *The Quest for National and Global Economic Stability*. In Honor of Hendrikus Johannes Witteveen. 1988
                                                                    ISBN 90-247-3653-6

* 17. D.E. Fair and C. de Boissieu (eds.): *The International Adjustment Process*. New Perspectives, Recent Experience and Future Challenges for the Financial System. 1989   ISBN 0-7923-0013-0

 18. J.J. Sijben (ed.): *Financing the World Economy in the Nineties*. 1989
                                                                    ISBN 0-7923-0090-4

FINANCIAL AND MONETARY POLICY STUDIES

*Published on behalf of the *Société Universitaire Européenne de Recherches Financières* (SUERF), consisting the lectures given at Colloquia, organized and directed by SUERF.

Kluwer Academic Publishers – Dordrecht / Boston / London